Toward a Reformulation of Natural Law

TOWARD A REFORMULATION OF NATURAL LAW

by Anthony Battaglia

Foreword by

James P. Mackey

THE SEABURY PRESS / NEW YORK

For Meredith

1981
The Seabury Press
815 Second Avenue
New York, N.Y. 10017

Printed in the United States of America

Library of Congress Cataloging in Publication Data
Battaglia, Anthony.
Toward a reformulation of natural law.

Includes bibliographical references.
1. Ethics. 2. Natural law. I. Title.
BJ1012.B38 171'.2 80-25362
ISBN 0-8164-0490-9

Contents

Acknowledgments vi

Foreword vii

Introduction 1

One / The Trustworthiness of Human Moral Reason 7

Two / Concerning Thomas Aquinas 26

Three / Seeking to Be Good 62

Four / Reason and Natural Law 81

Five / God, Morality, and Happiness 110

Conclusion 136

Notes 138

Index 149

Acknowledgments

In the course of writing and rewriting this book I have had the benefit of a great deal of very welcome advice. Victor S. Preller, Paul Ramsey and Gene Outka offered important help in the earliest stages. Subsequently the revised manuscript has been read and commented on by James P. Mackey, Paul Ramsey, Patrick Nichelson, James T. Johnson, Paul Menzel, John Crossley, and John P. Reeder. Their comments have been very helpful though I have not always followed their advice. Meredith Lee read the manuscript with a keen eye for textual clarity and intelligibility. Lisa Frieze was extremely helpful in preparing the manuscript. Such errors as remain are of course my own.

Foreword

Natural law—a brainchild of the great Stoic philosophers, with their faith in the divine rational principle, the immanent Word, the dynamic craftsmanlike fire, which would bring all things to their natural perfection; the envoy of the Roman empire builders in their practical need for a moral basis of legal obligation which could cross the boundaries of their polyglot lands; a god-send to the Christians whose founder had omitted to leave them a distinctive moral system, but who saw in the term "the Word" a natural bridge-term in their attempt to win over the pagans and at the same time to despoil them of their spiritual possessions; foundation of Roman law and thus of the main system of law in the Western world; as obvious a source of appeal for the American Declaration of Independence ("the law of nature and of nature's god") as it was to Paul VI when he wished to ban artificial contraception, not just for Catholics but for all men of good will. It has been for so long the foundation of moral theory and of civil law in the West that it would take a foolish person indeed to conclude that because it has run into some recent criticism, natural law is an obsolete religio-moral concept. If it has been abused—and it certainly has been—in ways which only its own specific nature as a philosophy of morals would allow, of what philosophical system of any length of tenure in human history can this not be said?

It is obvious in any case that in a religious tradition which can fairly be characterized as ethical monotheism the understanding and pursuit of the moral experience can never be in the least irrelevant to the future of that particular form of theism. Now, even the most perfunctory survey of contemporary Christian apologetics must see that at bottom it seeks to establish confidence in the reasonableness of the human spirit and confidence in this empirical world in which, in Heidegger's words, it is thrown, abandoned. In a more comprehensive phrase, the new apologists base their case for reconsideration of Christian faith in a so-called post-Christian era on man's ineradicable trust in the value of his present existence.

Human reason had been abused in the human quest for God in much the same way as the same human reason had been abused in the natural law approach to morality. For just as too many moralists thought they could read off from the most superficial description of natural organisms and processes the most immutable and absolute of moral prescriptions, too many natural theologians, as they were called, thought that God's existence could be proved by coercive logic from what seemed to them to be very obvious features of our empirical world. However, as this over-confidence in rather simplistic processes of human reason was gradually eroded by the philosophical posterity of Hume and Kant, and as it began to share in the common decline in this century of the general over-confidence in reason bequeathed by the Rationalist Age, Protestant Neo-orthodoxy's request for faith alone in God's revealed word and its extreme rejection of the aid of reason proved no more effective a strategy for restoring to Christianity even in the Western world its popular preeminence. In the view of Langdon Gilkey, already a father figure amongst the newest apologists—such is the exponential growth-rate of contemporary movements—neo-orthodoxy assumed too clear-cut a distinction between belief and unbelief, between the word of God and the secular experience of men and women. The world, he said, was inside the church, belief was saturated by secular doubt, and nobody was quite sure if a word from God had ever been heard at all.

As a result Christian writers from different churches and different countries, with few signs of collusion between them, have recently tried to find a way between hostility to old metaphysical certainties and indifference to pure Christian kerygma. Gilkey, Tracy, Ogden, Küng—even Rahner—for all the differences in their detailed methods of procedure, have all found it necessary to begin by appealing, as I have already said, to the reasonableness of the human spirit, despite its ambivalence, in its trust in the worthwhileness of this empirical existence, for all *its* ambivalence. So, without threat of logical coercion or of eternal damnation, an invitation is issued to commit ourselves once more to the rationality and the hope the human spirit has in the world. And along this route, it is asserted, God can once again be encountered.

Notice the prevalence of words such as value, worth, trust, commitment, in this new apologetic. Clearly in this latest enterprise to establish the ethical monotheism of Christianity, the basis of moral commitment is indistinguishable from the basis of belief. Yet the new apologists seldom if ever attempt to uncover this basis by means of a distinctively ethical approach. It is their most important corroborative effort—or, better, this equivalent, alternative exercise—which this present work of Anthony Battaglia supplies. In the present disarray of moral positions, just as much as in the present confusion of theological systems, the search for foundations is just as surely indicated. And it must be a matter of no small significance to the contemporary debate if, in his reading of the perennial point of natural law theory, Battaglia sees in it that same combined confidence in reason and reality.

It is no carping criticism of this new approach in either of its present forms—philosophy of religion or philosophy of morals—to say that its specifically Christian relevance, or the specifically Christian element within it, has yet to be irrefutably established. It is my own view that these basic philosophical approaches can establish the general form of the human possibilities of religious belief and moral commitment—and that this is an indispensable exercise of the human spirit—whereas the concrete matter and the impelling motivation of belief and commitment is supplied by those men and women in the course of human history who found these religious philosophies and keep them going and leave their own indelible stamp upon them as long as the human pilgrimage continues toward its uncertain future. But to say this is to ask for the next volume and not to take in the least from the welcome which this present volume has every right to anticipate.

James P. Mackey
University of Edinburgh

19 August 1980

Introduction

The question "what is morality?" is certainly not a new one; attempts to find an answer have characterized human reflection for centuries. Perhaps every possible answer has already been explored. Among the attempts to understand what it means for human beings to be moral is one of the oldest traditions, that associated with the term 'natural law.' In spite of the long history of that tradition, however, little attention is paid to natural law today outside the circles of Catholic moralists or students of jurisprudence. This book is an attempt to rescue the chief insights of the natural law tradition from this limbo to which it has recently been relegated. Before setting out on this task, however, it is worth examining why natural law is worth reconsidering at all.

Students of moral theory are aware that the status of morality is less clear today than it has been in most recent intellectual history. First of all, theories abound which reduce the claims of morality to mere subjectivity or entirely to the workings of psychological and social conditioning; such reductionism has a fatal effect on the enterprise of taking morality seriously. On the other hand, some theories explain too much: many traditional natural law explanations of morality could be cited as examples. Equally problematic are theories which stress too much human sinfulness. Fortunately, attempts have been made in the past decade or so to avoid these two extremes. Many of these attempts will be referred to later; they have in common an insistence on the reality of morals and they do so without attempting to completely explain all the workings of the human conscience. It is the contention of this book that natural law theory properly understood avoids the earlier extremes mentioned above and does so in a way that provides a framework in which recent, positive attempts to understand the meaning of morality can be expressed.

For more than anything else the natural law theory is a framework for understanding morality rather than a method for making moral judgments. The chief reason why natural law should be reexamined today is its usefulness as an explanatory paradigm of *what* morality is and *how* moral judgments are made. In spite of important theoretical attempts to free morality from models or explanations which claim for it either too little or too much we are still lacking a general theory which intelligibly roots morals in the ordinary experience of ordinary human beings. The first reason why natural law is worth looking at today is the promise that it can produce such a general theory for morality.

A second reason for reopening this topic can be found in the emphasis of the traditional theory upon public rules or conventions of conduct. Much modern ethical writing—I am using the words 'ethical' and 'moral' synonymously—concerns itself almost exclusively with the judgments of individual human beings. It is concerned with the ways in which individual persons become aware of the claims of morality and with the considerations that such individuals should bear in mind in making moral decisions. Such discussions are certainly important, for it is individual persons who act or do not act morally. Especially in a time in which moral consensus is shaky on so many matters attention to the concerns of individual moral agents is necessary. Still, such emphasis overlooks an equally important element of morality, the element of community moral standards. The collective judgments of individuals reinforce one another, and out of such reinforcement community standards emerge. Such community standards are hardly ever completely adequate for all individuals, but they constitute one of the most important factors in the making of individual choices. Moreover, the actions of communities, their judgments as incorporated into law or translated into political activity, are one of the most important arenas for morality itself. The natural law emphasis upon community standards, upon social norms and conventions and laws, is a needed corrective to an exaggerated concern with the individual and is a second reason for reopening discussion of that tradition.

One of the advantages of dealing with individual moral judgment is historical flexibility. In dealing with individuals it is possible, even necessary, to make allowances for the concrete circumstances of the agent. We are used to thinking that different persons arrive at differing conclusions about how to act according to the context of their action and their awareness of the factors which influence their judgment. Such flexibility seems to be only commonsense in dealing with individuals, and advocating it is certainly nothing new. In our time, however, emphasis on the need for flexibility at the level of the moral decisions of the individual seems often to be a way of avoiding talking about something else. Stressing the freedom of the individual bypasses the knottier issue of whether the problem is a more public one, of whether scientific and political changes have made the tried-and-true formulas of the moral conventions themselves questionable or inadequate. Allowing for the differences of individual moral judgment is not controversial; talking of change in public moral consensus is. We have all sorts of evidence that such change occurs—one example to which we shall return is the polygamy of such admired men as Abraham, Jacob, and Solomon, and examples closer to our own times are not hard to find. Discussion of change in morality is rare enough in religious circles, but especially rare in those concerned with natural law, for that theory has usually been taken to mean that such change is impossible. More than anything else this resistance to change constitutes a barrier to making sense of natural law. And therefore it is a third, and the most important, reason for reexamining the tradition.

The exposition of natural law which follows attempts to bring to that tradition the element of historicity. It is a reading of natural law which does not make claims for immutable moral precepts. Rather it sets the natural basis of morality in such a way as to make intelligible the changes in moral conventions which characterize our historical experience of the world. Such a historical understanding of natural law has been the hope of many sympathetic to the tradition but conscious that past formulations have allowed only the merest crevices for such change. This study hopes to fulfill the wish of such thinkers (John Courtney Murray, for example) to see natural law formulated in a way that respects human historicity.

For these three reasons an examination of the natural law tradition seems sorely needed. The first two reasons have been part of the traditional understanding of natural law and will probably come as a surprise to no one. The third, however, historicity, is less familiar. In fact if the natural law tradition is to be understood in the context of history a great deal of its scholastic carapace will have to be left behind. Precisely because some readers will think that this shedding of medieval categories does violence to the tradition, attention is paid here to the work of the greatest of natural law theorists, St. Thomas Aquinas. In attempting to begin a reformulation of natural law I have made use of many categories derived from him. However, my reading of Thomas is not the one familiar to many readers of this essay. It is, admittedly, a revisionist understanding of Thomas Aquinas although I have usually preferred to use the word 'appropriation' in discussing my use of his formulations. Revisionism has become an acceptable word within the Catholic theological community, but I do not lightly hide behind that label. However unfamiliar, my reading of Thomas Aquinas is grounded in his texts and can certainly be read as a valid understanding of his thinking.

In the book that follows I begin by stating the meaning I attach to the expression natural law. The term has overtones of meanings which must be rejected—most readers for example will be happy to learn that I do not defend a concept of metaphysical natures. Still, natural law seems the most adequate term to describe the exposition of morality which follows. Even without a Neoplatonic doctrine of nature, the essential claim of natural law remains, after all, a metaphysical one, however problematic such a metaphysical claim may be. In this respect natural morality carries the same burdens as natural theology, and I examine this parallelism briefly.

The greatest part of the exposition of Thomas Aquinas is included in the second chapter. I am concerned there to interpret Thomas' statements of the nature of our knowledge of morality in line with his understanding of our knowledge of the truth. 'Truth' is a category which Thomas treated at far greater length and much more often than the category 'good,' but his more extensive treatment of our knowledge of truth applies equally well to his understanding of our knowledge of good. Since Thomas maintained that our knowledge of the former was an analogy, the same must also be said of our knowledge of the latter. Secondly, the two places in which Thomas speaks of natural law at some length are placed in context with one another. His earlier understanding of natural law differs a great deal from that he expounded in his last work, although the difference has been often overlooked. In any case, Thomas avoids in the latter some of the more pressing objections which have been formulated against natural law.

The three remaining chapters each deal with an essential element of the natural law tradition. In Chapter Three I propose a version of Thomas' contention that the principle 'good is to be done and evil is to be avoided' is part of the ordinary knowledge of ordinary human beings. The explanation of this principle derives not from Thomas, however, but from more modern philosophical and social scientific categories. It is essential to the natural law tradition that ordinary human beings ordinarily want to be good. Such an essential part of human consciousness need not be stated in medieval categories but can be expressed in a terminology more familiar to us.

Another essential element of the natural law theory is the assertion that the requirements of morality can be known through the use of human reason. The fourth chapter examines this claim. Chapters Three and Four in fact are an explication of the essential claim: human moral reason is trustworthy because it is in touch with reality. This claim has a corollary assertion: we ought to act as we think we ought to act. Chapter Four then examines what we know about morality as a result of our reflection upon reality. It is here that the elements of constancy and variability in the expression of a natural law morality are discussed.

Although the book does not deal explicitly with most of the theological objections to natural law, some of these are dealt with at least indirectly in Chapter Five. The more mystical claims of religion share with philosophical skepticism a tendency to put morality into a framework so vast as to make it incomprehensible. However, a third essential element of natural law theories, at least to Christians, is the assertion that what God requires of us is that we act according to reason. That human reason is an inadequate receptor of the knowledge of ultimate reality is a constant of religious traditions, yet the assertion made above stands. The final chapter examines this paradox but acknowledges the theological element in it, an element which does not create the paradox but may be the only way of resolving it. In any case the chapter concludes with a repetition of one of the chief points of the book as a whole—assertion that in moral matters human reason means *moral* reason and that moral reason is grounded not only in external reality but also in the mysterious recesses of our knowledge of what it means to be a human person.

ONE

The Trustworthiness of Human Moral Reason

A book about natural law has a formidable array of problems to contend with. Hardly a topic in moral thought seems more exhausted than that of the natural law tradition. The idea behind that phrase has meant many things at various times in our intellectual history, but today few moral theorists seem willing to take any of them seriously. The reasons for this are many. A widespread awareness of cultural diversity, for example, has made it hard to take any given set of norms as 'natural' to human beings. Philosophical problems abound, as do theological ones. A whole book could, in fact, be constructed around objections to the idea of a natural law for human morality. This, however, is not such a book. Many objections to natural law theories seem to be valid and many of the defenses of such theories seem to be defending the wrong thing. Arguably at least, both attackers and defenders of a notion of natural law see in that tradition a claim for a kind of knowledge—of natures or apodictic truths or principles—that I do not wish to defend.[1] Instead of engaging in the pros and cons of this discussion I would like to present an alternative view of natural morality, in continuity with the tradition but not, I think, open to the kinds of objections made in the past.

As a point of departure one might look at some of these. The chief objection seems to be the one that centers around the issue of naturalism; at least, this is the chief one with which this book shall be concerned. This problem arises because natural law theories have in common an assertion that morality is based upon reality, and this seems to open the door to insuperable problems. For most of this century philosophers have tried to state the basis of morality in a way that would avoid what has been called the 'naturalistic fallacy'. That fallacy has been defined as the identification of goodness with a natural property of things; and its opposite, that goodness cannot be derived from the natural world, has been one of the slogans of recent moral philosophy. The terms of this discussion were set by G. E. Moore and have had a devastating effect, among philosophers at least, on attempts to assert a natural basis for morality.[2] And yet, in retrospect, it seems that Moore's main intent was to assert the independence of morality from scientific, especially social scientific, attempts to preempt it.[3] In that respect he seems to have been reacting to some of the excesses of the late-nineteenth-century world of his childhood. Catholics who grew up with the detailed certainties of the old moral theology handbooks may well understand such a reaction. He might also be said to have been echoing the famous distinction between 'is' statements and 'ought' statements first formulated in those terms by David Hume more than a century before him. Most of the moral philosophy of this century has been dominated by this assertion of the independence of moral language—in either Hume's language or in Moore's—and yet as the century comes to a close it is sometimes hard to see why these formulations have been so much of a fixation. In any case, the reformulation of natural law that follows does not, I think, run afoul of these problems.

This is not to say that it would be easy once again to defend a notion of the natural basis of morality. Certainly it is as difficult now as at any time in the past to defend a notion of simple naturalism, though one occasionally does find an argument using the categories of natural law which does so. Indeed, the most famous context in which the phrase 'natural law' occurs in common use today—that of the issues of sexual morality and of sex roles—is an egregious example. But to speak of such naturalism is not necessarily the same as talking of natural law; at the least it is not the only way to do so. Part of the problem of any attempt to reformulate natural law, in fact, is that the issue could be approached in so many ways. The question of naturalism must be faced. But there are a number of other philosophical questions which might also be attended to; to cite but one example, the question of whether a natural law ethic must presuppose the existence of God. In most cases questions such as this will be dealt with only by implication, if at all, for the model I am proposing does not seem to necessitate raising some of the issues or to be vulnerable to the others. The complicated issues of the epistemology of individual decision making are also not dealt with because the model is intended to represent a high level of generality. Theological objections to natural morality, on the other hand, are left unanswered for other reasons. Many of them raise questions far more complicated than natural law alone; for example, the whole issue of the meaning of grace. As for other objections, before they can be approached, one must know what one is defending when defending natural morality. This essay hopes to help establish just that.

Natural law theories have traditionally asserted a metaphysical claim, a claim that metaphysical reality is such that human morality is grounded in it. This does, in fact, seem to be the essential claim that characterizes a theory of morality as part of the natural law tradition. But this essential point, hard enough in itself to explicate, is frequently obscured by being cast in a language from a previous era. Some of this vocabulary must have been difficult to understand even centuries ago, and it survives in the modern world only as a caricature. In the past, the natural law claim might have been stated in language such as "any law which has a binding force flowing from the very nature of things prior to any knowledge or determination by a human legislator is called natural law."[4] Such language now seems excessive. The more modest formulations of a thinker like John Courtney Murray are frequently overshadowed by such statements. Murray himself was an able taxonomist of the caricatures of natural law. Among those he lists are "abstractionism," "intuitionism," "legalism," and "immobilism."[5] Almost anyone who takes up the issue of the natural basis of morality today is aware of these and similar problems, but as yet no one seems to have found a way around them.

The Meanings of 'Nature' and 'Law'

This study will not concern itself with direct rebuttal of the criticisms of natural law which have been put forward in the recent past. Most of these criticisms have been correct. Unfortunately they are associated with the term natural law itself and for this reason I use the term with some hesitation. The word 'natural' can have three meanings. In the first it is distinguished from 'supernatural'. In the terms of a distinction in Catholic theology, natural law is not a matter of special revelation; it is not something that can be known only through the Scriptures or in faith in Jesus Christ. Rather it is a part of general revelation, a way of knowing which can be confirmed by, or supplemented by, special revelation but is not dependent upon it. A somewhat more secularized version of this meaning is that natural law is natural in the sense of being ordinary; it is part of the ordinary experience of human beings and, as such, is common to us all. Morality is natural to humans in this sense. This assertion of what the word 'natural' means in 'natural law' is not problematic and everything in this study is consistent with it.

A second meaning of the word natural is that associated with the technical term 'naturalism' and is frequently referred to as the 'naturalistic fallacy'. This 'fallacy' is the assertion that goodness can be defined as a natural property of a thing or action. As has already been noted, those who term naturalism a fallacy frequently associate it with the 'is/ought' distinction. The latter is the assertion that moral language is logically distinct from descriptive language, i.e., that there is no strictly logical connection between a description of a situation and what I ought to do in that situation. These are matters of logic and of definition and are, I believe, acceptable as far as they go. They are, however, sometimes taken to mean that moral language is subsequently meaningless or at best merely subjective, that is, not founded in reality. The status of moral language is indeed problematic, but there is no logical entailment between the earlier fact about the distinctiveness of moral language and the latter assertion of nonreality. On the other hand, of course, it also may not be possible to logically prove that morality is founded upon reality and is therefore 'natural'. This study does not restate natural law in a way that commits the naturalistic fallacy or violates the is/ought distinction. In fact, its distinctiveness lies in its acknowledgement of the problematic nature of moral language while nevertheless asserting that morality is founded upon reality.

Two time-honored ways of maintaining the real basis of morality while nevertheless avoiding the linguistic confusion of the naturalistic fallacy or the is/ought problem have been 'intuitionism' and what has lately been called 'non-cognitivism'. Each has distinguished proponents today. John Rawls' *A Theory of Justice* has done a great deal to make the former position philosophically acceptable again.[6] (Even though G. E. Moore, the famous proposer of the naturalistic fallacy was an intuitionist.) Rawls believes his own notion of "justice as fairness" is intuitively true and further thinks that intuitionism "holds that no constructive answer can be given to the problem of assigning weights to competing principles of justice. Here at least we must rely on our intuitive capacities" (p. 40). In extreme forms, the other alternative, non-cognitivism, "claims that an ethical judgment is not a true or false ascription of any property to anything, but something very different, like an interjection, a command, a wish, a resolution, or a prescription."[7] In other words, non-cognitivism plays down reason and is frequently not concerned with a realist basis for morality. But William K. Frankena, from whom the preceding quotation comes, is both a non-cognitivist and holder of a position which he calls "ethical absolutism." His own version of non-cognitivism is "that what carries the 'normal member of our society' from the factual premises involved to his ethical conclusion—and does so reasonably—is not necessarily any Ought premise, nor any rule of inference, but simply his moral concern for others, his sympathy, or his commitment to the moral point of view" (p. 145). The difference between Rawls' intuitionism and Frankena's non-cognitivism may not be as great as might at first appear. Both seem to assert the real basis of moral judgment and are opposed to considering morality as arbitrary. The intuitionist sees its origin in an intellectual perception, while Frankena's non-cognitivist emphasizes the commitment of the will to "the moral point of view."

Rawls' concept of the origin of principles of justice and Frankena's understanding of the basis of moral judgment have in common an understanding that even though we must use to the maximum our rational abilities, in some sense we cannot explain the origins of morality. Rawls uses the metaphor of a "veil of ignorance" behind which principles of justice are chosen (p. 12). Frankena asserts that we cannot say "Morality requires . . ." without taking a "moral point of view" (p. 181). Frankena associates his position at one point with that of St. Thomas (p. 145) and indeed Thomas can be read in Frankena's way. He has also been read as an intuitionist—texts can be found to support both positions—but it does not seem necessary to make a choice. Both positions can be subsumed in a category that is used by a third modern moralist, Daniel C. Maguire, the category "mystery." For Maguire, "the foundation of morality is *the experience of the value of persons and their environment*. . . . Moral debate takes place because persons are perceived as valuable in such an exquisite way that a world of awe and oughts is born in response to them. Ethics exists as an effort to see what does and does not befit persons in all of their marvelous and compelling valuableness and sacredness."[8]

As can be seen, Maguire is not afraid to speak of the "sacredness" at the heart of the origin of moral experience, or later to speak of it as "mystifying" and "mysterious" (p. 74). Such language is open to the charge of vagueness, of course, and, in fact, the burden of Maguire's book is an attempt to specify the conscious, mostly rational, aspects of moral choice. But the book is concerned with the more general point that morality is natural in the sense of real, and that an open admission of the mysteriousness of the relation between reality and morality is necessary. Like Maguire's work, this essay leans toward non-cognitivism rather than intuitionism but it would be a mistake, I think, to reopen an argument over the primacy of intellect or will in the mysterious recesses of the human soul where moral language is born.

A third sense in which the word 'natural' can be understood in the phrase natural law is 'according to the nature of things'—where the word 'nature' is not used in the sense in which we use it in ordinary discourse, the general sense of 'ordinary'. Rather it refers to the notion that things in the material world have fixed 'natures' and that these are unchanging, and are normative for human beings in a moral sense. Much natural law reasoning in the past has proceeded from this assumption, and it is this association of the word 'natural' that makes the idea of natural law so open to attack today. Thomas Aquinas himself defined natural law in this way early in his life but, as we shall see, he had mostly abandoned it in his later writings. The vocabulary of 'natures' conjures up a stable, fixed world, impervious to change and history. The present study has no interest in this particular understanding of the world and therefore none in this particular sense of the phrase natural law. I see no need to defend the idea of natural law against attacks upon this discarded meaning. As John Courtney Murray realized, a way of formulating the notion of natural law must be found that respects the historicity of human experience of the world.[9] In such a formulation the notion of unchanging nature seems to have no place.

However, this matter is far more problematic than is frequently realized. We may find it easy to be critical, or even slightly patronizing, toward Thomas' attempt to make moral judgments on human sexuality—in an age far different from our own. But some future generation may find our appeals to our own ideas about the world to be just as objectionable. Inevitably in trying to make sense of *how* to act, it is necessary to use data about the world *in which* we act and about what it means to be a human agent. Our preferred definitions—or assumptions—of the way the world 'really is' or the way human beings 'really are' come from different sources than Thomas'. We may prefer data provided by psychologists, or ecologists or (heaven help us!) sociobiologists—but it is hard to avoid making the same formal 'mistake' as did the early Thomas. At the least, it is difficult to avoid being as culture-bound. In trying to reformulate natural law as we shall be doing in the remainder of this book, it is not enough to avoid the naturalistic fallacy. We must at least try to understand how data about the natural world are used in a moral way.

Some of the problems of the word 'law' in the expression natural law are directly related to those of the word 'nature' in the third sense given above.[10] Like Platonic natures, natural laws have been seen as fixed and unchanging as, for example, in the quotation from *The Dictionary of Moral Theology* given above. Much like political laws they had a kind of propositional form—as commands or precepts—and seemed to allow no room for human freedom or autonomy, much less for change or history. I see no reason to defend such a propositional notion; to the extent that it is ineradically bound up with the expression 'natural law' the expression is useless and as bound to a past era as the Roman numeral system. But an element of the denotation of law is implicit in the claim that morality is based on reality. When we speak of an autonomous, historical understanding of morals—as we must if we are to make sense today—we are not saying that morality is arbitrary. An autonomous, historical morality is one which humans discover in their own experience of the world and of other persons in it. But a true morality is an appropriate response to that experienced world and its inhabitants, and that appropriateness is not determined simply by one of the parties to the interchange. This is to say simply that the appropriate response to needless suffering that can be stopped is never merely whimsical or arbitrary. Though the word 'law' conjures up too great a surrender of human autonomy, and this is problematic, not all of its overtones can be done away with.

The problem can be resolved if we remember that the word law is an analogy. (We shall look at Thomas' notion of analogy in the next chapter.) We continue to use this analogous sense in talking about the 'laws of science', although we may tend to think of the meaning of the word law as the descriptive one, 'occurring with predictable regularity'. In the natural sciences the predictability aimed for is total (as it also is in mathematics and logic). And though some developments in the twentieth century (Gödl's Theorem, Heisenberg's indeterminacy principle) have indicated the limits of such an aim, these sciences do achieve a remarkable degree of rigorous predictability. In the social sciences, on the other hand, the degree of predictability which is achieved is of a statistical kind, frequently stated in rather round terms. ("In most cases . . .", "in a significant minority of cases . . .", "the ordinary reactions," etc.) The claim of Thomas Aquinas was that the moral response of persons to a given situation was of the latter kind. His Latin phrase *ut in pluribus* can be translated into English as 'in general' or 'in the long run'. His contention, and that of the natural law tradition in general, is that widespread agreement can be achieved *ut in pluribus* on moral judgments of a high degree of generality, but that consensus becomes harder and harder to achieve the more one moves from general judgments to particular cases. This particular kind of predictability is a necessary part of natural law theory and a later chapter shall be devoted to it.

Thus the expression 'natural law' is a problematic one. Both of its elements contain meanings that must be rejected, even though these meanings may be the ones which first come to mind on hearing the expression. On the other hand, both words contain meanings that must be affirmed if any modern theory is to be in continuity with the past. I have no particular brief for the expression, but no short alternative either. I prefer to say 'morality is based on reality' but the expression is clumsy to use. Frankena's 'ethical absolutism' does not seem preferable, as 'absolutism' has as many problems as 'law', while Maguire's 'ethical realism' sounds too much as if one were trying to avoid optimism or pessimism ("Let's be realistic!"). This book uses a number of such expressions, but the use of 'natural law' should be heard, if possible, without its problematic meanings.

The Premise of Natural Law

Is there a way of stating the core premise of natural law theories without raising the problems we have promised to avoid? I think there is. It is: *That human moral reason is trustworthy because it is in touch with reality.* But though this double premise is the heart of the tradition, there is a corollary to it that is more familiar to us and should be first attended to. If human moral reason is trustworthy, then *we ought to act as we think we ought to act.*

In the language of Thomas Aquinas this corollary is stated as "we ought to act according to reason"—*hoc rectum est et verum ut secundum rationem agatur* (*S.T.*, I-II, Q94, A4). This conclusion is, for all practical purposes, why he finds natural law useful; the chief exception, as already noted, is the moot one of sex ethics. Throughout the special ethics section of the *Summa* (II-II), natural law is used chiefly as an appeal to human reason. Some modern commentators have argued, in fact, that this corollary is all of natural law that can survive the transfer from the language of the thirteenth century into our own. Even if this were so (and I do not believe that it is) a revival of natural law would have a profound influence on the practice of the Christian Church. H. Richard Niebuhr quite rightly criticized the tendency of natural lawyers to mean by "according to reason" nothing more than "what seemed reasonable years ago." It is all too easy to state natural law theories in ways that seem to commit us to a given metaphysics or anthropology rather than to human reason. When such a metaphysics or anthropology ceases to make sense the only way in which its moral language can be defended is to make it a matter of faith, of revelation, or of obedience to authority. And this is to make it no natural law at all. On the other hand, of course, notions of what seems reasonable are subject to manipulation, and are all too frequently just obedience to a different kind of authority—to an advertising campaign, or to a pundit, or to the *Zeitgeist.*

Still, it must be emphasized, trust in the ability of human beings to know what they ought to do is what makes natural law *natural.* Moral perception is part of the ordinary processes of human life; it is natural and it is trustworthy. The natural law tradition is thus committed to a rather optimistic—or, more accurately, not pessimistic—understanding of human beings. But to assert this is not to forget that the tradition also asserts that morality is in touch with reality and that reality is no more plastic to us in moral matters than it is in any other way. The other side of the natural law assertion that humans can know what they ought to do is the assertion that, in the long run, some choices "work" and others do not. As Camus put it: "The Greeks never said that the limit could not be overstepped. They said it existed and that whoever dared to exceed it was mercilessly struck down. Nothing in present history can contradict them."[11]

The premise of the natural law tradition, that human moral reason is trustworthy because it is in touch with the real, is a strange proposition to try to explain. We might first look at what it does not mean. The premise does not say what the real is, though there is a constant temptation to think we have figured out such a description: Platonic forms or history on the march; the dance of Shiva or the love that moves the sun and the other stars; patterns of psychological or sociological necessity. Perhaps we cannot do without such stories but the stance toward morals we are speaking of does not commit us to a particular world view but rather to the seriousness of moral perception. In this thin form the tradition adds nothing to human awareness and does not explain it; it is not necessarily intuitionistic. From this point of view the stories we give ourselves to explain our moral awareness, be they precepts of law or theories of alienation or sublimation, are less important in themselves than as aids in recognizing the utter seriousness of moral reason.

Without a story about what reality is, this will be a much "thinner" version of natural law than some readers may expect. But this is no more than such a theorist of natural law as John Courtney Murray claimed for it. "It can claim only to be a 'skeleton law', to which flesh and blood must be added by . . . the rational activity of man, aided by experience . . ."[12] Before proceeding to the remainder of the theory, however, some recognition should be made of the implications of the basic premise. It is in two parts: that human moral reason is in touch with reality, and that it is trustworthy. Let us look first at the notion that moral reason is in touch with reality, which is the metaphysical, or ontological, claim of the premise.

Natural Law and Natural Theology

The problem that this view of morality poses is roughly the same posed by natural theology. The latter has also increasingly been under fire, although it has even more defenders than has natural morality. But it is to be expected that natural morality and natural theology would have roughly parallel epistemological problems. One of the chief problems for natural theology has been that posed by Immanuel Kant. He inaugurated a revolution in philosophy by emphasizing that what we call reality must be understood to be at least partly the result of the human mind's ordering of what must, to an infant say, be the chaos of sense experience. Kant tellingly used his understanding of human knowledge to attack the ontological argument for the existence of God and with it all natural theology. In its earliest form the ontological argument was a proposal that certain concepts of the human mind—'being' or 'perfection', for example—implied that the thing referred to existed outside of the human mind, or they could not be real being or real perfection. The argument has undergone many permutations, but the essential shape of its premises has remained.

Paul Tillich summed up the argument thus: It is

> . . . the rational description of the relation of our mind to Being as such. Our mind implies *principia per se nota* which have immediate evidence whenever they are noticed: the transcendentalia, *esse, verum, bonum.* They constitute the absolute in which the difference between knowing and known is

> not actual. This absolute as the principle of Being has absolute certainty. It is a necessary thought because it is the presupposition of all thought.[13]

Tillich says of this "rational description" that it is not an "argument" and, in fact, Kant's criticism remains cogent. Granted that our minds are not mere mirrors of the world outside us, we have no way of examining reality itself, but only our ideas about reality.

Nevertheless, one finds that the claims about reality do not go away. Recently some social scientists have come close to repeating the basic moves of the traditional argument. Robert N. Bellah's assertion, "religion is true," is the clearest example I know in which a social scientist implicitly espouses the ontological argument. Made in a controversial address to the Society for the Scientific Study of Religion, the statement is placed in the context of a plea for a fuller epistemology than the prevailing one with its relegation of human meanings to 'mere subjectivity' and thus to unimportance. Drawing on Michael Polanyi, Paul Tillich and Talcott Parsons, Bellah is defending the reality of symbolic language, a position he calls symbolic realism. However one evaluates such an attempt to rethink our epistemological prejudices, the reader will still be struck by the similarities between Bellah's assertion and the classical moves of the ontological argument.

It is certainly within the province of a social scientist to suggest that religion is a constant of the human condition, that, for example, the need for meaning is universal or that persons cannot usually live as though the universe is simply chaotic. What distinguishes Bellah's proposal from the usual analysis of the social scientists is that he did not say that religion is *real* but that it is *true,* a claim that seems far beyond the capacity of sociology, or any other human discipline, to make. For it is one thing to assert that religion really exists as a constant of the human condition, and quite another to assert that the claims of religion are true, that there is in fact a meaning to human life. It is this stepping beyond the confines of what we can safely assert about reality outside the human mind that seems to parallel the claims made, more abstractly, by classic proponents of the ontological argument. It may, however, be unfair to tax Bellah with too little philosophical rigor; he is arguing that religion is a phenomenon *sui generis,* and attacking what he sees as a real epistemological shortcoming of his profession. Nevertheless, his example is instructive by its very excess.

Not only theorists of religion are laying the ground work for an understanding of the human condition that moves beyond reductionism; influential theorists of psychological explanations of the human condition are doing so also. Here, even more than among social theorists of religion, a diversity of positions have been taken. And although they have much in common (a denial of utopianism, an attack on reductionism), their diversity is such as to make generalization difficult. Out of a group that might include Norman O. Brown, Philip Rieff, Robert Lifton, and James Hillman,[14] we shall choose one author who cites all but the last of them approvingly, Ernest Becker. Becker's *The Denial of Death*[15] was a best seller and prize winner in spite of its variance from some of our cultural prejudices and of its linguistic confusion in philosophical and religious matters. Using Brown's work and that of psychologist Otto Rank, Becker argues that the root psychological problem for humans is that of finiteness, that we are not strong enough to live happily with the wonders of life nor with its terrors, especially the terror of non-being. Inevitably, then, we must find someone or something outside of our physical bodies that will justify our condition, someone or something onto which we can 'transfer' our desire to overcome the limitations of humanity. One of Rank's insights that Becker is able to use to great effect is the way in which artists and writers are able to transfer onto their own works, which will remain when they are gone, and are therefore able to give the appearance of not needing to transfer at all. Into this situation, that is, given the inevitability of transference, Becker interjects, as a social scientific question, the issue of *where* is the best place to transfer?

> We have to look for the answer to the problem of freedom where it is most absent: in the transference, the fatal and crushing enslaver of men. The transference fetishizes mystery, terror and power; it holds the self bound in its grip. Religion answers directly to the problem of transference by expanding awe and terror to the cosmos *where they belong* (p. 202, italics mine).

Becker proclaims the "closure of psychoanalysis on Kierkegaard"—who emerges from *The Denial of Death* as one of "the surest giants in the history of humanity," (p. 259). Becker agrees with Rank that "man is a 'theological being'," not a biological one (p. 175), but unlike Bellah he is locked into an epistemology which is incapable of sustaining the insight. On the one hand religious belief is an 'illusion,' a community-sustained 'myth' (Becker uses 'religion' and 'myth' in their limited senses, at variance with the reconstruction Bellah, for one, is trying to make), yet on the other hand he talks about the best transference as onto "God," "the cosmos itself," and "the life force" as though these were synonyms. His is an instructive example. On the one hand, the logic of his argument is that of Augustine's "our hearts can never rest until they rest in Thee," and yet his empiricism cannot be comfortable with his conclusions. Such a dilemma may be one of the intellectual characteristics of our time and from it perhaps derives some of the book's force and success. But here again, although in a more muddled way, we see the attempt to move logically from assertions about human beings to assertions about the universe, from the realities of the human mind to the reality of God: the ontological argument one more time.

For here is the problem. Suppose that human beings are such that "the orientation of men has to be always beyond their bodies, has to be grounded in healthy repressions and toward explicit immortality ideologies, myths of heroic transcendance" (Becker, p. 285). Suppose that the "need for a truly religious ideology . . . is inherent in human nature and its fulfillment is basic to any kind of social life" (Rank, in Becker, p. 174). Suppose that we are in fact unable to live without a sense that life is meaningful, that "God is not mad." Suppose that humans need meaning, value, self-transcendance and that these needs (or this need, perhaps) are a fact about human beings—a social scientific fact—the best hypothesis given the available data. Are not all of these suppositions no more than modern ways of saying what Anselm and Descartes and Hegel said when they formulated the ontological argument, once we allow for the fact that the classical version was more concerned with the logical necessity of explaining concepts rather than with grounding more generalized human needs? We might call these new formulations statements of an 'inevitable need' of human beings but are they not simply equivalent ways of talking about what was earlier called an 'undoubtable idea'? And are not all these new formulations just as susceptible to the time-honored objections to the argument? The bind is such that it is not surprising that the social sciences have been so long in coming to this understanding of human nature and that we should not be surprised that such is not yet (and perhaps not likely soon to be) the accepted premise in these supposedly value-free disciplines. For in this new version, the standard objection to the ontological argument takes a new form, a poignance and desperation that we do not hear in discussions of the logical status of the verb 'to exist.' It is this: can we trust the human mind? Or worse: how can we know that we are not dinosaurs?

Dinosaurs, of course, were an evolutionary 'mistake'—a dead end. Their adaptation to the world was dramatically successful for a while, but in the long run their massive physical size could not be supported by the environment and they disappeared. We cannot *know* if our nervous systems, like the bodies of dinosaurs, are hypertrophied; if they demand more from the world than it can give. At any rate, the prospect is not one we like to consider. Like the question "Can we trust the human mind?"—which cannot be coherently stated, much less answered—this rejection of the ontological argument reveals to us the limits of our knowledge in a way that traditional rejections do not. For, as the data of the argument switches from abstruse philosophical speculation to empirical data about human beings, then the fact that such a line of reasoning does not "work"—cannot stand up to the most rigorous logic—assumes a hollowness, and fearsomeness, it seems never to have had before. No longer a philosophical abstraction, it has become a central humanistic concern. And it is a concern that takes us to the limits of our knowing, for there is clearly no way that we can step outside the human mind to see if it is in touch with reality 'as it is'. This impossibility has long been the backbone of objections to the ontological argument.

Thomas Aquinas also rejected the ontological argument—although he accepted natural theology! Thomas' rejection of the ontological argument is the usual one: actual existence is not proved by mental states (*S.T.* I,Q1, ad 2). But he is not unaware of the need to posit the ultimate trustworthiness of the human mind.

He does so not as a philosophical assertion (as if it were something that we could reasonably know) but as a theological one. The ultimate grounding of the human mind lies in what he calls participation in the divine mind. That is, as Thomas understands the Christian faith, it provides grounds for trusting, in a limited but real way, the necessary assumptions of the human mind.[16]

The premise of the present study is that we can trust the human mind, that human beings do indeed belong in the universe, that we are not *de trop* or absurd, that we are not dinosaurs. To choose otherwise may be possible but it is not easy. I do not wish to press here the implications of this difficulty, except to insist that trusting in the congruence between the meaning of being human and reality itself appears to be natural to human beings, and thus to be a defensible, though not a provable, understanding of human moral judgment.

This book follows the line of certain natural law theories in acknowledging that morality is ultimately based on reality, but my hope is to make that claim credible without attempting to go much more into metaphysics or epistemology to try to defend it. Morality is a mystery and it is one which we can demonstrate, but not explain. By comparing natural theology and natural morality I wished to draw attention to their similarity. Perhaps, at their very bottom, they share a kind of shadowland which some say proves they are reasonable, while others say the shadowland can only be crossed by faith.

The Trustworthiness of Moral Language

The second part of the basic premise is 'human moral reason is trustworthy'. This is really neither an ontological nor an epistemological claim. For both of these categories are matters of that part of human reasoning which Thomas called speculative—that is to say, they are concerned to describe the way things are. But natural law is after all a matter of moral language and the real usefulness of its claims seem to be not descriptive but moral. Part of the essential claim of the natural law tradition is that human moral reason is trustworthy. To say that it is trustworthy is only partially a descriptive claim; the real descriptive claim is contained in the assertion that our moral judgments are in touch with reality and this, together with the question of trustworthiness as a logical problem, has already been spoken of. The element of trustworthiness is a moral element. This other part of the basic premise can be accurately rephrased as 'our moral judgments ought to be trusted'—and if they ought to be trusted then they ought to be acted upon. This specifically moral element has three aspects to it. The first two of these are made clearer in the corollary.

The logical consequence, or corollary, of the basic premise of natural law theories, can be thus stated: we ought to act as we think we ought to act. For most modern readers the importance of this corollary is probably its statement of the freedom of the individual human conscience. As we hear this corollary we are likely to attend most specifically to the dependent clause and especially to the assertion that it is our judgment as *we think* that ought to determine our moral actions. This aspect of the natural law tradition has already been mentioned. Others may hear in this corollary to the natural law premise a way of asserting the independence of moral language from descriptive language. How *we think we ought to act* is determined by moral considerations and cannot be reduced to a mere description of the external world. In this case I do not think my version of it adds anything to the more traditional version: 'we ought to act according to reason', but this version has the advantage of emphasizing that it is moral reason that is being referred to and thus bypasses the misreading of the traditional formulation which mistakenly says that there is some way of using ordinary descriptive language to automatically describe the moral thing to do. (There is a price to be paid for thus bypassing the problems associated with the is/ought distinction and the 'naturalistic fallacy', as the reader shall see later.) Both of these ways of reading the assertions 'Human moral reason is trustworthy because it is in touch with the real', and 'We ought to act as we think we ought to act', are important not only for the analytically minded, but also for anyone caught in a dilemma between personal judgment and community standards. In the latter case, especially, it is worth emphasizing once again that this primacy of conscience is built into all of what follows, but that it is not the intention of this book to deal with individual judgments except as they are shared by groups of persons and thus become matters of *community morality*.

But neither of these ways of reading the essential premises of natural law theory get at what may be the most important element of these premises. This element is perhaps the most specifically moral of the features of natural law. It is, roughly, that morality is a matter of the utmost seriousness. We shall see later the sense in which morality or the practice of morality seems to be built into the consciousness of what it means to be human. In fact the natural law theory takes for granted that morality is a constant of human consciousness and that it is a serious matter. We shall see that Thomas believed that all human beings have a sense that "good ought to be done and evil ought to be avoided" and we shall have to examine the meaning of a statement which seems so perplexing on the face of it when one looks at the moral confusion and even corruption of the world around us. But what I am calling attention to here is a broader element, one that the natural law tradition tried to formulate. It is an element which may be so obvious that a counter example will be useful. Theories have abounded in this century which have reduced moral language to the expression of mere conditioning, whether psychological or social, or to the simple expression of emotion, theories epitomized in Ayer's too often referred to (and too much attended to) dictum that moral statements are 'meaningless'. Clearly, in all of these theories, and most especially in the last, there is a denial of the seriousness of moral reason. Undoubtedly those who put forward such theories were morally serious in one sense of that term (which shall be discussed in the third chapter), but their formulation indicates that they themselves have narrowed and have encouraged others to narrow the rightness of that seriousness. It is unfortunately all too easy to limit the seriousness of moral claims either in respect to our reflection on what we ought to do or to the degree to which we actually do it. But from the perspective that moral reasoning is grounded in reality, all theories about morality must be judged morally. One element of such a judgment must be the degree to which any given theory encourages persons to limit the seriousness with which they attend to moral matters. In other words a third important element of the statement 'We ought to act as we think we ought to act' might be expressed by saying that we ought to think about our actions and we ought to act on the judgments we make. Such a perspective is commonly that of the preacher or the psychologist or someone directly concerned with motivating persons. But human motivation does not exist independent of other elements. One important contributing factor is the intellectual framework which persons use to interpret themselves and their place in the world around them, that is to say, how they interpret what morality is, and in this the philosopher's contribution is important.

Of course such a framework can encourage or discourage moral seriousness. And of course moral seriousness of itself is not enough. It must be informed and reflective and in touch with the real world; be "prudent," as Thomas Aquinas would say. This book is not directly concerned with motivating persons but rather with matters of analysis and description. Nevertheless we must acknowledge at the beginning that one of the chief claims of the natural law tradition is that morality does not occur in a vacuum but rather that it is a way of dealing with reality and a matter whose seriousness cannot be tampered with except at the cost of losing touch with the real world.

TWO

Concerning Thomas Aquinas

Natural law has such a long history and so many interpreters that anyone who picks it up ought to be conscious of what tradition his own theory resembles. In the chapters that follow, I will be suggesting a version of natural law which parallels, although it may not exactly duplicate, one of the versions of that tradition found in Thomas Aquinas. But although his name was one to conjure with as recently as fifteen years ago, Thomas Aquinas is a problematic figure right now. For generations, but especially in the first half of this century he had been taken as the definitive interpreter of the Roman Catholic tradition, but he is so no longer. If we have learned one thing from the twentieth century and from Vatican Council II, it is that a static Neo-Platonist understanding of the world must be rejected as inadequate; and Thomas' eminence has subsequently plummeted. Nowadays both Catholics and non-Catholics who have been used to the extraordinary weight attached to his opinions as recently as twenty years ago are likely to find the invocation of his theories tiresome, to say the least. Nevertheless, it is in his second theory of natural law (and I will soon explain why I number it second) that I find the most adequate classical expression of the foundation of public morality. And so recourse to this thirteenth century thinker seems worthwhile.

Before discussing some of the features of Thomas' understanding of the basis of morality, it is worth our time to be clear that the present book is not an historical study. Whatever Thomas meant in the thirteenth century, whatever his combination of the Bible, Christian Platonism and Aristotle meant in his time, it is unlikely to have much relevance to ours, except as it has been translated out of a cultural perspective far different from that of a man who lived before the scientific revolution, the European discovery of America, and the awakening of the modern sense of history. In what follows I am less concerned with the "historical Thomas" than with certain understandings of the moral enterprise which can be found in the work of that figure from the now distant past.[1] A persuasive argument can be made, I am convinced, that much of what we have learned to identify as Thomas' understanding of natural law is really the interpretation of such early modern thinkers as Suarez and Victoria rather than an explanation of Thomas.[2] What is about to follow will seem an unusual reading of Thomas to those who have been schooled to read him through the eyes of such figures as those. But this point reinforces our enterprise in two significant ways. On the one hand, the late sixteenth-century commentators who revised Thomas according to their understanding of the late Renaissance world were doing no more than I am attempting to do here. They were attempting to make sense of a profound thinker whose world view they no longer shared. They believed that their recasting of his ideas remained true to his earlier insights, but they recast them in terms comprehensible to their own times. On the other hand, the works of Suarez, Soto, Cajetan and the like can now be read not as commentaries on Thomas but as an example of a unique kind of late scholasticism; their relationship with Thomas does not exhaust their own historical interest. In other words, Suarez and the others interpreted Thomas in somewhat the same way that he interpreted Augustine and Aristotle. Just as he was less concerned to understand Aristotle as a fifth-century-B.C. Greek than as a person who had had some insight into the truth, so they (Suarez, Soto, etc.) interpreted Thomas. Douglas Sturm has called this procedure "appropriation" and he means by this term what might be called, in a kind of shorthand, remaining true to the insight rather than to the historical setting.[3] The idea is not unique to Sturm. I have already said that in practice it can be found many centuries ago, that Thomas appropriated Aristotle, and the verbalization of the practice goes back at least to John Henry Newman.[4]

Appropriating the past should not be taken to mean being untrue to Thomas. My hope is the opposite, to remain true to him while showing the contemporary relevance of his ideas. I am not claiming that everything to be found in subsequent chapters is to be found in the thought of Thomas Aquinas. I hope that what cannot be found there is compatible with Thomas' thought, once allowances have been made for the changes seven centuries have brought. In the chapter following this one I shall take up a description of the origin of moral language which is, as I have said, consonant with the one Thomas proposes in the *Summa Theologiae* I-II. There we shall have to talk of the foundations of moral language in the human desire to be good and subsequently of the ways in which that fundamental drive is institutionalized in moral language. There, as in the rest of this book, I am concerned with proposing a viable model of natural law, rather than with Thomas Aquinas himself. But in this chapter I am concerned with him and the way in which he deals with three aspects of natural law.

One of these aspects, the most essential one, is the analogous, or reformulable, status of our knowledge of the good, and of morality in general. The others are less vital points, but help to show that even in his own terms, Thomas recognized some of the modern "problems" of natural law theory. They include the development of Thomas' ideas of natural law and his way of distinguishing moral language from descriptive language. Readers who have had their fill of thirteenth-century thinkers, or are already persuaded of this previous point, may decide to proceed immediately to the next chapter. Those who continue on here should be forewarned that Thomas consistently proceeds in his arguments as a Christian/Theologian, and as one who lives in and shares a Neo-Platonic or Aristotelian world view. This fact provides him with a perspective with many metaphysical and theological presuppositions. The chief of these is that one begins talking of 'truth', 'law', etc., in the certainty that one is dealing with a universe that a Creator has created good. The focus of Thomas' attention is this Creator and this world thus assured of goodness. This ought not to surprise us, of course, but it needs to be said because it has consequences for this study. It means especially that Thomas begins at a different place than the argument of the rest of this book, and he does so with a vocabulary that may today seem baffling: "divine ideas," "the knowledge of God," etc. In some ways the vocabulary is a carapace for natural law theory today and it is our hope to free it from this time-worn shell. But Thomas' understanding of the limits of human knowing seem to remain valid, though we might go about making the same points differently.

In the section which follows we shall be looking at the understanding of human knowledge which Thomas enunciates in his treatise *de Veritate.*[5] As the reader shall see, Thomas was more aware of human intellectual limitation than we might have expected, but the reader should not be surprised to find that he expressed this awareness in a vocabulary quite foreign to us. In spite of the vocabulary of "divine ideas," etc., Thomas has a quite profound understanding of just how limited our knowledge is. In a subsequent section we shall examine Thomas' first theory of natural law, which he developed in the *Commentary on the Sentences of Peter Lombard.*[6] The theory of natural law which most interests us is that of Thomas' later work, the *Summa Theologiae,* but completeness requires that we examine the earlier theory to see why both Thomas and a modern reader must move past it. Finally, this chapter will examine Thomas' understanding of the "good" for human beings and its relationship to that unknowable happiness for humans which is God.

Analogy and Reformulability

The word 'analogy' has a long tradition of usage among religious thinkers. Philosophers of religion use it, for example, to locate our ideas about God in a middle position that make them not entirely adequate to what 'God' means, but not entirely inadequate either. For Thomas Aquinas analogy is also the category by which he explained the relative adequacy of ordinary human knowledge. Only occasionally is he concerned with its relative inadequacy. For the purposes of this book, however, it is this latter aspect of analogy that most interests us. If human knowledge is at least partially inadequate, it is to that extent possible to reformulate what we know. Reformulating means, in its commonsense usage, to say the same thing in a different way. However, such a definition of reformulation is loaded, and the reader will note that I am using it as a justification for the appropriation of which we have been speaking. Analogy entails the possibility of reformulation; the two are the same thing, seen in different ways. If we have not noticed this enough in the past, it is undoubtedly because, whatever the theoretical possibilities of reformulation, the practical difficulties of actually doing it are so great that no one would think of attempting the task unless he was forced to. Philosophers, for their part, now speak of the reformulability of all human language and so have invented a kind of secular equivalent to analogy.[7] The need for such a concept is clear. As our understanding of historical change and cultural variability becomes greater, the more conscious have we become of the inconstancy of human certitude, the vagaries of truth.

Thomas Aquinas could be amazingly agnostic at times. Especially in his early writings, there is an emphasis on the unknowability of God which seems more appropriate to a mystic vowing silence—to John of the Cross counseling *Nada*—than to a man who wrote endlessly about God for the fifteen or so years of his productive life. He was capable of writing, for example:

> When therefore we proceed to God by way of remotion, we first deny of him anything corporal and then we even deny of him anything intellectual, in the sense that it may be found in creatures; and so also 'goodness' and 'wisdom'; and then there remains in our minds only the notion that he *is,* and nothing more; wherefore he exists in a certain confusion for us. Lastly, however, we remove from him even 'being' itself, as that is found in creatures; and then he remains in a kind of shadow of ignorance; by which ignorance, in so far as it pertains to this life, we are best conjoined to God . . . and this is the cloud in which God is said to dwell.[8]

It is a continual amazement how from such darkness, so much agnosticism, so much creative theology could flow. It is possible to imagine that he changed his mind, or that he spoke sometimes as a philosopher, sometimes as a theologian, or simply to question his consistency. I think that none of these explanations is correct and that there is a more historical solution that is both simpler and more difficult.

Thomas, we remember, is the man most responsible for changing the vocabulary of Christian language about God from Augustinian platonic language to Aristotelian. It was a profound and fruitful exchange. Only if we think such profundity comes cheaply can we fail to realize how deeply Thomas must have gone into the mystery of God to have found the freedom to make such a change. The wonder, of course, is that he returned. Many who make that journey do not. Thomas himself, at the end of his life, is said to have lost interest in his own masterpiece, the *Summa Theologiae,* and retreated into silence. "It looks like straw to me," he is reported to have said. *Mihi videtur ut palea.* The quotation given earlier is proof that this perception of the *ultimate* inadequacy of human language was one that he had lived with for years. The sense of the uselessness of language to perfectly express truth of the human condition may be a useful experience if one is going to be able to do what Thomas did, to translate from one cultural language into another. As we shall see, if it is true for Thomas that we cannot speak clearly of God, it is equally true that we cannot speak clearly of the 'good'.

The suggestion I wish to make is that perhaps a washing clean, an evacuation of categories of the past, is a necessary first step in the changing from one set of categories to another. It is precisely because language is ultimately useless when referring to God or 'good' that we are tied to the less-than-ultimate partial usefulness of any particular language or cultural scheme. Once we have seen that no particular set of human categories is truly adequate, we are free to use the partial adequacy, partial inadequacy of human language wherever we find it.

If we approach Thomas' writings from this perspective, and I think we must, we must do it with a curious double vision. On the one hand we must remember that all language about God and, by extension, about his creation, is inadequate, analogous, reformulable. On the other hand, in Thomas' language, it is also true that we participate in the creativity and spontaneity of God, that grace does not replace or destroy our human nature, it perfects it. Or as Thomas More says in the Robert Bolt play, "God gave us wits that we might serve him wittily."[9]

For our modern consciousness, of course, to state the problem of knowledge in this way is to begin at the wrong end. Our experience of our own freedom and creativity does not need to be affirmed as the mystery of God. We find ourselves free and creative in this world and we have hope in a God who will make our freedom worthwhile. But at whichever point one begins it is the double vision that matters, not the statement of it.

Thomas asserts that even though human knowledge is only analogous, it is nevertheless in a very real sense true and trustworthy. In order to say this, it is necessary for him to ground human knowledge in the creation of a good God. Because we are creatures of a good God, we can be confident that the human mind participates in the divine mind.[10] Concretely, we can be confident, that the beginning of human reasoning, a key term in Thomas' argument, is, in fact, a participation in the real. What does Thomas mean by the beginning of human reasoning? He means the fundamental principles of reasoning, principles so fundamental that we cannot question them without, in fact, using them. These principles are given to us with the divine assurance of their correctness. For Thomas, this means that the knowledge of first principles, as he calls it, in the speculative intellect is in fact grounded in the real. These first principles are what we today would call the rules of logic. Thomas consistently uses the following example: A thing cannot exist and not exist at the same time. With regard to the practical intellect, or practical reasoning, Thomas thinks that the principle, 'Do good and avoid evil', which he sometimes calls *synderesis,* is of an equally unquestionable certainty. As we noted in the first chapter, such things cannot be known philosophically. It is, in fact, uncanny that Thomas saw this, and saw that participation is a necessary but theological category, not a philosophical one.[11] It is as a consequence of this theological certainty that Thomas can say that our knowledge of the world is "real" knowledge, but, nevertheless, analogous knowledge. Thomas nowhere explains his doctrine of analogy at any length, but it is enough for us to remember that analogy stands, for him, between univocity, or simply identity, and equivocity, or complete distinction. Our knowledge is not univocal with the way things are, for this is the way in which they are conformed to the mind of God. To know things in this way would be to know the mind of God—a patent, absolute impossibility for creatures. "To know a creature in the world in this manner is to know, not the creature, but the Creator" (Ver Q 8.a.16, Reply).[12] On the other hand, our knowledge cannot be equivocal either, for this would violate the goodness of God; it would mean that nature was useless—a theological and philosophical impossibility that Thomas never takes seriously. No, our knowledge is analogical—neither wholly true nor wholly false—somewhere between univocity and equivocity.[13] The exact placing of our knowledge between these two extremes is likely to be described by different commentators on Thomas in different ways. In principle, however, analogy is correlative with reformulability. For what is only partially known can be known differently, though still only partially. The exact degree of reformulability is, I think, less important than the primary fact that analogy entails reformability.

Thomas has good theological reasons for claiming that the expression 'natural law' refers to something, but he has difficulties both theological and epistemological in claiming that we can know this something we refer to as natural law. The distinction between the ontological claim and the epistemological one is a crucial one, and one that Thomas well knew. The difficulty arises because natural law is, in one of its senses, the harmony between creation and the mind of its creator; as such it has an epistemological status identical to the status of 'truth' for Thomas, and quite similar to the status of our knowledge of God himself. Thomas does not shy away from talking about our knowledge of 'truth' anymore than he avoids talking of 'natural law', but he does both of these only after having constructed an ingenious and subtle set of quotation marks around the terms. The problem is a surprisingly modern one, except that instead of asking about the relationship of our ideas of the world to the world itself, as a modern philosopher might, Thomas asks of the relationship between what we know with our minds to what God knows. The difficulty we have in unraveling what Thomas is saying in his thirteenth-century vocabulary is an example of why it is important to unravel it. Thomas is talking about the limited, partial nature of human knowledge, a limitation we encounter to some extent as we try to move from culture to culture. Our difficulty in following Thomas' vocabulary thus arises out of the same kind of human limitation that he is trying to describe.

As might be expected, Thomas believes the world to be God's creation and to be known by Him. The way the world really is, from such a point of view, is the way it is known to be by God. But God not only knows the world, he also wills it into existence. In talking about the world as known by God, Thomas uses expressions such as "divine ideas," whereas when talking about the world as willed by God, he speaks of "eternal law." Neither of these expressions is part of our common vocabulary today. Nor is it common today to talk of a distinction between a human speculative intellect, whereby we know truth, and a practical intellect, whereby we know goodness. But something important to the understanding of our moral knowledge is entangled in these terms. Since the point is an important one, it seems worthwhile to clarify its place in the Christian tradition and thus this section adheres more to Thomas' language than will the rest of this essay.

There are remarkably few places where Thomas talks of natural law in itself. Where he does discuss it, however, he usually puts it in context with the beginnings of "speculative reason" and thus draws a comparison between our knowledge of truth and of goodness. To this we shall turn in the next section.

Law and Truth

In regard to human knowledge, Thomas distinguishes between the speculative and practical intellect, although he maintains that the distinction is with regards to ends, and not a distinction in the intellect itself, which is one. The speculative intellect deals with the consideration of truth, the practical intellect with operations towards an objective. The one has the habit of *intellectus principiorum,* the other that of *synderesis.* Both are habits men naturally have, according to Thomas, and both are necessary to explain man's relationship to the world around him. *Intellectus* and *synderesis* function both as explanations of how we know and of how we know that our knowledge is related to what God knows, that is, to what really exists.

Before we can look at these terms, however, another parallelism must be examined, one frequently overlooked but very important to the understanding of natural law. For Thomas both our knowledge of natural law and our knowledge of truth depend on our relation to the divine ideas. As a result, the way in which he sets up a discussion of our knowledge of natural law is the same as that in which he sets up our knowledge of truth. At the beginning of his discussion of law, Thomas asserts that eternal law is the name we give to the governance of the universe by God:

> . . . law is nothing but a dictate of practical reason issued by a sovereign who governs a complete community. Granted that the world is ruled by divine providence . . . it is evident that the whole community of the universe is governed by God's mind. Therefore the ruling idea of things which exist in God as the effective sovereign of them all has the nature of law.[14]

The eternal law, then, is equated with the ideas in the divine mind as these are promulgated, or willed into existence, by God. Because all things conform to the idea that God has of them, these ideas function as law for the "whole community" of the created universe. Thomas is, of course, using the term law analogously here. In fact, both 'eternal law' and 'natural law' are analogous terms in at least two ways, one rather obvious, the other less so. The divine ideas are the law of the universe, in the sense that the universe does, in fact, conform to them. There is no possibility that it could do otherwise. From our point of view eternal law is law only analogously because it is a description of a state of affairs rather than a prescription of one course among several open to the universe. From God's point of view, however, it is law proper, for it is prescriptive of this set of states of affairs and no other, even though other possibilities might have been chosen. The description of natural law as a state of affairs, as descriptive rather than prescriptive language, is one of the analogies involved here. The second, less obvious analogy to which I wish to call attention, is the analogy that exists between our language about God and God's language. This analogy is but one example of the general analogy this section sets out to show.[15]

In addition to 'eternal law' and 'natural law' the other important analogous term in this passage is the more ancient one of 'divine ideas.' Thomas adapts it from the Neo-Platonic tradition, and, especially, from Augustine. For the latter, the divine ideas were the "forms of things" which exist separate from the things, but not separate from the Creator. In Augustine's epistemology the notion of divine ideas not only served to explain how the Creator knew his creation, but also figured importantly in the explanation of how it is that we know truth. By a kind of illumination we come to know the divine ideas and thus know the forms of things. Thomas rejects Augustine's illuminationism, but continues to use his language regarding the divine ideas as something immanent in God. Some such notion seems to him a necessary consequence of the conclusion that God's knowledge includes knowledge of his creation.[16] Instead of Augustine's illumination, however, he uses the notion of participation and the specification of that participation is the function of the habits of *intellectus principiorum* and *synderesis*.

By introducing the term 'law' into the discussion of the conformity of the universe with the "divine ideas," the analogous term we have developed, Thomas is setting up a framework in which he will be able to carefully distinguish eternal law, natural law, human law, etc. Distinguishing only offhandedly between God's providence as *knowledge* and God's providence as *will,* he presses on to the distinction of kinds of law. By setting up the distinctions in this way, however, that is by identifying law with the divine ideas, he has not only described eternal law as immutable, but has also created a problem about how man could know it. It is a problem he addresses more directly in dealing with truth. In setting out the distinctions between eternal law, natural law and human law, he is reusing the formula he has already worked out for important, and parallel, distinctions regarding truth.

The distinction of different meanings of truth occurs several times in Thomas' writings, but nowhere more clearly than at the beginning of *de Veritate.* There, dealing with the speculative intellect, Thomas sketches (more briefly than we would wish) the problem of how much of what goes on in our minds is the same as what is contained in the mind of God. The sketchiness of the discussion is one consequence of Thomas' not treating systematically the question of analogy. Had he done so, this passage would have been less difficult. He proceeds here in a manner identical to that which he uses in the discussion of law. Just as *law* will be defined in such a way as to make it possible to see in the divine ideas the ultimate law, so *truth* is similarly defined. Law is "a dictate of practical reason issued by a sovereign who governs a complete community"; and the universe conforms to the divine mind. So truth is the conformity of intellect and things and all things conform to the idea of them in the divine mind.[17]

> If truth in its proper sense be taken as that by which all things are primarily true, then all things are true by means of one

> truth, the truth of the divine intellect . . . But if truth in its proper sense be taken as that by which things are said to be true secondarily, then there are many truths in different minds about one true thing. Finally if truth in its improper sense be taken as that by which all things are said to be true, then there are many truths for many true things, but only one truth for one true thing.[18]

If Thomas were using the vocabulary he adopts with regard to law, he might call this conformity of the universe with the divine mind 'eternal truth'. That he does not should not obscure from us the similarity in the two concepts. In order to keep straight the several senses which Thomas gives to the word truth, I shall adopt this modification and use the terms eternal truth and human truth where Thomas uses "primary" and "secondary." The distinction between the two is that whereas things conform to ("are measured by") the divine intellect, our intellects conform to the things. Between the two intellects, conforming to the one and causing the other to conform to it, is the thing to which Thomas feels we can ascribe truth in a real, but improper sense. This real but improper use of truth is the only sense in which things can be called true. Since properly it resides only in the mind as conformed to the thing, truth cannot properly be used as a predicate of things. However, since they are *real* ("have being") to the extent to which they conform to the divine mind, they can be called *true* to that same extent. This analogous use of true, which seems unimportant to us, is important to Thomas for metaphysical reasons; he wants to be able to say that *being* and *truth* are convertible. It does not bother him at all that such terms are only analogous.

The pattern is tripartite. 1) God knowingly creates things and these things exist as true inasmuch as they are known by God. This is the primary, proper sense of truth—*eternal truth.* 2) Things, inasmuch as they conform to the divine mind, can be called true in an improper, analogous sense, even though truth is properly a matter of knowledge. 3) Our minds conform themselves to the truth inasmuch as they conform to the thing; truth exists properly, but secondarily in our minds—*human truth.*

In the first question of *de Veritate,* Thomas is revising Christian theology in accordance with an insight he learned from Aristotle. Nothing is in the mind (our mind, that is) unless it is first in the senses. In order to incorporate this insight into Christian theology, he must get rid of the notion that our minds are enlightened by the divine ideas, as Augustine taught, without giving up the two notions that God knows his creation and that we know the world. The two-level theory of truth is his way of solving this difficulty. This solution has several important features. We come to know truth by coming to know the thing, and not independently of things. It is the thing which is the standard against which our sense of truth is judged, not the divine idea of the things. Consequently, we come to know the thing, not the proper truth of the thing, which is its relationship to the divine mind.

This last point must be constantly kept in mind if one is to avoid reading Thomas' theory of knowledge as if it were a simple-minded abstractionism by which we easily come to know eternal truth. For a variety of philosophical and theological reasons, Thomas does not believe that we know the truth-of-things, that is, the way in which the thing conforms to the intention of God. Our knowledge is only partial knowledge because we know of things only what our senses tell of them, and *our senses cannot grasp the way in which things are true.* We know things by their similitudes, not by their essences, he is careful to say when pressed.[19] He is not always concerned with such distinctions, and as a result one must always check in any given context which of the various senses of truth he is using.

The difficulty of the schema that Thomas suggests is that it leaves open the question of the relationship of what we know to proper truth. The distinctions Thomas has made would be unimportant and hardly new—the similarity to Neo-Platonism is clear enough—if Thomas were to take the avenue of solution open to Augustine. If we are, by divine action, enlightened by the divine ideas, as Augustine taught, then the gap between eternal truth and human truth could be seen as a difference of degree rather than kind. Thomas' Aristotelianism prevents such a solution, but he avoids the danger of positing the opposite extreme, of saying that there is no relationship between eternal truth and human truth.[20] He posits, instead, a habit natural to man which is a "knowledge of first principles." This habit, *intellectus principiorum,* he calls a sharing in the divine light; it assures that our minds operate through a participation in the divine mind. We shall see later that this solution is a far more tenuous one than it appears at first glance. *Intellectus* may then appear as an assurance, theologically justified and philosophically necessary, that our minds conceive reality in a mode appropriate to creatures and that is enough for Thomas.

On the other hand, we should note that Thomas thinks that the ideas of things as they exist in God are identical with the creative essence of God and that "to know a creature in the world in this manner is to know, not the creature, but the Creator," a knowledge we do not now have.[21] At this point questions about our knowledge of the truth of things—the way in which they conform to the Divine intention of them—becomes a question of our knowledge of God himself. As a result, the fact that we do not know the truth of things does not bother Thomas very much. It would be contrary to our status as creatures to have such knowledge. He is convinced that man has all the advantages and limitations of being a creature. Thus his knowledge will be in a creaturely mode and will be adequate for his creaturely needs, but there is no possibility that his human intellect will be able to grasp the creative essence of God. Even the angels have "morning knowledge"—knowledge of things as they exist in the divine mind—only as a result of grace and not as a power of their own intellects.[22] The knowledge man has of God is, at best, only analogous to his knowledge of the world and the status of this analogy is not without its own difficulties.

Though Thomas continues to use the word 'truth' to refer to what the human mind knows, we should note that the primary meaning of that term is what God intends when he intends the world. The secondary meaning of the term truth, namely, what we intend when we intend the world, is patently a different intention (although the degree of difference is not clear). Thomas continues to call both intendings true because of the formal nature of truth—conformity of intellect and thing—but we should not quickly assume that even the mode of that conformity is the same. It is, in fact, clear that the key analogy in this matter is that of the conformity of things to the divine mind as analogous to the conformity of our minds to the thing. The analogy of truth does not rest in a distinction in the thing known, but in the mode of knowing the thing.

Joseph Pieper, whose essay "The Negative Element in the

Philosophy of Thomas Aquinas" seems to have been the first to notice this strand of Thomas' thought in recent times, lays great stress on our creaturely status and its consequences when speaking of the limits of our knowledge.[23] Pieper correctly points out that for Thomas the problem shows itself in the fact that we can form no concept of being and that thus we know that there is something very important about reality for which we do not have any but circular terms. Pieper's explication of this negative element is to lay great stress on the knowability which exceeds the powers of our minds, rather than to speak of unknowability. Because, to know things in their very being is to know them as they conform to the mind of God, they exceed our grasp, although we can continue to learn more and more about them. The human intellect knows the world around it, but its knowledge is always capable of deepening and improving . Our knowledge may be adequate for us, but it will never, until the vision of glory, be adequate for the things which are reflections of the divine mind.

This formulation of knowability which exceeds our powers is the way Thomas puts this point on several occasions, although on other occasions he speaks as though truth were a univocal rather than an analogous term. In dealing with this aspect of Thomas' thought Victor Preller's adoption of the vocabulary of languages is apt.[24] Preller proposes to refer to God's intentions of the world as a language. The truth by which things are conformed to God's intellect—God's intention of the thing—is adequately known only in a postulated "language of God." That which we call language, corresponding to our human intentions of things, is less than wholly adequate because of the creaturely nature of our intellects; although it is adequate for us as creatures. Without using this modern vocabulary, Thomas returns to this distinction and the limitations it forces on us again and again in casual reminders that we do not know the nature of things,[25] for example, in his distinction of the angels' morning and evening knowledge, and in his discussion of the acquisition of human knowledge by Christ, who already knew the divine ideas. He consistently maintains that there are at least two "languages" in which to refer to things: the human and the divine.[26]

The importance of the distinction to the development of a natural theology in Thomas is quite clear. The difficulty of making significant reference to God in human language has led many theologians and philosophers to attempt to reformulate Thomas' epistemology in order to shed more light on his natural theology. Without pursuing the line taken by such studies any farther toward natural theology, we can still see that the fundamental claims about human intentionality's inherent limitations, postulated by Karl Rahner in a phenomenological mode and by Victor Preller in an analytic one, have sound basis in Thomas. His claims for human truth are not nearly as strong as we might be led to suspect. Nothing in human intentionality is exactly the same as it is from God's point of view, and a perfect human intention of the world is not possible for man *in via.* The creaturely status of man's knowledge means that we do not know anything except in terms of *our* knowing power and that we are unable to make truth claims about the way things *really* are, as God knows them, but only about the way they are to us. This is clearly the old problem of the relation of what we know to the thing which we know. How do we know that what we represent to ourselves in concepts, words, etc., is what really is outside of our minds? The question is in some sense unanswerable. If there are things "out there" that do not appear in our conceptual system, they must be of no importance to us because they obviously do not affect us. Yet, it is at least possible that our concepts are really at variance in significant ways with the things to which they are supposed to refer. Thomas does not want the gap between human knowledge and divine knowledge to be unbridgeable, and so he introduces into his epistemology an assurance that there is at least an analogy between human truth and divine truth. This assurance is a theological one, in that it cannot be derived from any observation of the conformity of our minds with God's, but only from non-observational belief. This theological assurance he enters into his epistemology as *intellectus principiorum.*

The "habit" of *intellectus principiorum,* as Thomas calls it, provides us with exactly that, the knowledge of first principles. These first principles, roughly the fundamentals of logic, are prior to any argumentation or real knowledge and are absolutely necessary as a starting point of human reason. *Intellectus principiorum* is a habit we have by nature and the principles we come to know by this habit are a sharing in the divine intellect.

The extent to which this habit assures our ability to know the way things really are is not entirely clear in Thomas. He relies heavily on the notion of analogy without anywhere systematically explaining the exact meaning of the term. This problem is universally recognized in discussions of Thomas' natural theology, but rarely has sufficient account been taken of the ways in which even "ordinary" metaphysics, and all of philosophy, is modified by Thomas' theological caution.

It does not seem necessary for the purposes of this discussion to attempt to construct an understanding of analogy that would be adequate to cover all kinds of human knowledge. Suffice it to note that all human knowledge is in theory reformulable.[27] We shall return later to the way in which Thomas modifies his epistemology with the concept of *intellectus*. We should simply note now that the assertion that man has an ability to share in the uncreated light of the divine intellect has the peculiar status of a theological statement, rather than a philosophical one, based on Thomas' belief in the goodness of creation. The issue of our mind's ability to know the world is, of course, a common philosophical one. Even this postulated theoretical ability does not change Thomas' mind about the nature of human truth, since the mode in which we receive this "light" is our human mode, which is not sufficient to let us know the "natures" of things. Thomas was well aware of the limited use he was making of this enlightenment of the human intellect, even though he handles it gingerly, because it seems to set him against Augustine, with whom he is usually at great pains to give the appearance, at least, of agreeing.

> But that Augustine did not understand all things to be known in their eternal types or in the unchangeable truth, as though the eternal types themselves were seen, is clear from what he says–viz. that "not each and every rational soul can be said to be worthy of that vision," namely of the eternal types, "but only those that are holy and pure" such as the souls of the blessed.[28]

This passage is especially notable because Thomas is stretching Augustine to fit Thomas' own theories. It is Thomas' interpretation that only the blessed in heaven have knowledge of things through the eternal types, and it is only by careful interpreting that he is able to have Augustine agree with him.

That our status as men *in via* has these consequences for our grasp of truth has obvious importance for the understanding of Thomas Aquinas, consequences widely overlooked until fairly recently. I have been developing this line of Thomas' thought at some length because he is much more concerned with our ability to know the truth than with our grasp of the good. It is in this former category that he works out most carefully the consequences of his epistemology, although all the distinctions he makes with regard to truth are present in his discussion of that which the practical intellect knows: natural law. The speculative and practical intellects are, after all, the same intellect, and the limitations described for the one are bound to be the same as those of the other as well. The difficulties presented are identical, and Thomas' solutions to the difficulties are also identical, although Thomas does not sketch out the identity at any great length.

Before we go on to look at the parallels between the distinctions of truth and the categories of law, however, we should note that in a strict sense the case we set out to make has already here been made. Inasmuch as thinking about morals takes place within our human intellects, it has the same necessarily analogical status as any other human thought. If we know only in our limited human mode, then that is that. Further amplification of this point by examination of the practical intellect is, in theory, unnecessary, but it seems useful to pursue the point to the end.

Synderesis

We have already seen that both eternal truth and eternal law refer to the ideas in the mind of God. Because the world conforms to God's intentions of it, those intentions are both true and regulatory. Because God's intentions of the world are identical with his creative essence, they are unknowable by us in our present state. This unknowability seems to have bothered Thomas less with regard to truth than it did with regard to law. While he was content to have man using only his own language as a way of getting around in the world, he seems at first glance to have made more substantive claims about the law for man. Upon examination, however, we find that Thomas has indeed preserved his parallelism. He only *seems* to be giving more to the practical intellect than he was willing to give to speculative intellect. Because he is not so concerned with law as he is with truth, he moves much faster and the quickness of his transition from the unknowability of the eternal law to talk about natural law can lead us to believe that he is making stronger claims than his whole epistemology or theology would, in fact, allow him to make. Unfortunately, also, he blurs the distinction between synderesis and natural law, using one term where he has need of two. The result is a confusion that could easily have been avoided and which can be rectified by a closer attention to the status of natural law in Thomas' own theological system. Once the distinction between synderesis and natural law is carefully drawn, it is possible to see that Thomas is being quite consistent and, as a result, is really making far fewer claims for our knowledge of the natural law than he appears to be. His basic claim is not that we *know* the natural law, but that there *is* a natural law. We are governed by it, we participate in it and—in a limited way—it is knowable to us.

The greatest difficulty in the interpretation of natural law in Thomas has been the reading which has placed natural law solely within the practical intellect. This difficulty arises because of Thomas' own use of terms. Whereas when speaking of truth he carefully distinguished eternal truth, the truth of things, and human truth, in a tripartite distinction that has already been discussed, Thomas uses only two terms here: eternal law and natural law. Although he was careful in talking about truth to make sure that there could be no passage directly from the divine mind to the human mind, but only inasmuch as both are conformed to the truth of things, one perfectly, the other imperfectly, he here seems to be allowing for the possibility that there is no middle term between eternal law and natural law. This is the reading of natural law that is implicit in many discussions by students of the "Thomistic" school. In fact, the middle term is not missing for Thomas himself. This passage must be quoted in full:

> Law is a rule and measure . . . and therefore can exist in two manners, first as in the thing which is the rule and the measure, second as in the thing that is ruled and measured, and

> the closer the second to the first the more regular and measured it will be. Since all things are regulated and measured by Eternal Law, as we have seen (91, 1) it is evident that all somehow share in it, in that their tendencies to their own proper acts and ends are from its impression.
>
> Among them intelligent creatures are ranked under Divine Providence the more nobly because they take part in Providence by their own providing for themselves and others. Thus they join in and make their own Eternal Reason (*unde et in ipsa participatur ratio aeterna*) through which they have their natural aptitudes for their due activity and purpose. Now this sharing in the Eternal Law by intelligent creatures is what we call natural law.
>
> That is why the Psalmist after bidding us "Offer the sacrifice of justice" and, as though anticipating those who ask what are the works of justice, adding "There may be many who say, 'Who will [show] us any good?' " makes reply, "The light of thy countenance, O Lord is signed upon us," implying that the light of natural reason by which we discern what is good and what evil, is nothing but the impression of the divine light upon us.
>
> Accordingly it is clear that natural law is nothing other than the sharing in the Eternal Law by intelligent creatures.[29]

Several parts of this passage require examination. First, however, the similarity between this passage and a passage in *de Veritate* is of utmost importance:

> . . . natural things from which our intellect gets its scientific knowledge measure our intellect. Yet these things are themselves measured by the divine intellect, in which are all created things—just as all works of art find their origin in the intellect of an artist. The divine intellect, therefore, measures and is not measured; a natural thing both measures and is measured, but our intellect is measured, and measures only artifacts, not natural things.[30]

The language of these two passages is similar enough to make clear that Thomas is in both cases talking of the same kind of relationship with the divine intellect. In Thomas' notion, it is man himself (a natural thing) who is measured by the divine intellect, not man's intellect. Man's intellect gets its knowledge from his study of the thing, not from some sort of infusion by the divine intellect. And importantly, Thomas does not make an exception to this schema even in the case of man's knowledge of himself. In a famous passage, Thomas notes that we have the same kind of knowledge of ourselves as we have of things outside ourselves, knowledge based on observation. It is by observing our own acts that we come to know ourselves, in the same way as we understand other things, and we know other things "not by their essence but by their similitudes."[31] Thomas notes in this passage that it is easy to conclude that we must have a knowing power because we find ourselves knowing things, but it is very difficult to know the nature of the human mind. In fact, as regards the latter, much subtlety is required and "many are ignorant of the soul's nature and many have erred about it."

Thomas thinks, then, that there is indeed a conformity between man and the divine intention of man and that this conformity "measures" man. Because man conforms to the divine intention of him, this divine intention is the law for man. Since law is an ordinance of reason, for Thomas, it can exist only in minds—just as truth can exist only in minds. As something which resides in God it is eternal law, as something which resides in man it is natural law, but between the two minds, again, there is the thing. And just as Thomas manufactured a third term, the 'truth of things' to explain the status of truth in things, so he might have manufactured a third term to explain the status of law in things. At times, Thomas seems to want to use 'natural law' itself as this middle term. When he distinguishes natural law and precepts of natural law, or natural tendencies and our knowledge of them,[32] he seems to be moving natural law into the status of what we might rather call the law of things. The question is once again that of the relation of *our knowledge* of our conformity to God's will to the actual conformity we have to it. The ontological status of law is exactly the same as that of truth and, we shall see, their epistemological status is exactly the same.

We saw earlier that Thomas' solution to the dilemma posed by the inability of man to know either eternal truth or the truth of things was to postulate the existence of a natural human habit, *intellectus principiorum,* which was a knowledge of the first principles of speculative reason, even though it did not overcome the fact that we know things in their similitude rather than in their essence. In the passage the *Respondeo* of which I have quoted in full, Thomas introduces a similar notion with regard to the practical intellect. He does so, however, in a most peculiar way. It is this paragraph, beginning "That is why the Psalmist . . . ," and the consequent uses of the same notion in question 94, which has led to many of the problems of natural law in Thomas. The first difficulty that faces us is the absence of the notion of *synderesis.* According to the pattern he uses everywhere else with regard to the divine ideas, Thomas could consistently distinguish between our conformity to God's will and the sharing we have in it by divine enlightenment. He should not use the same term to cover both this conformity and the enlightenment of our minds. As a matter of fact, he does use this distinction of terms in discussing the powers of the intellectual soul.[33] There he uses the term *synderesis* to describe the ability of man's practical reason to have a starting point in fixed principles, a starting point given by divine enlightenment and equipping us with a set of first principles of the practical reason, much like the first principles of the speculative reason. Further, the same wording which here refers to *synderesis* as it enlightens our practical intellect can be found in a reference to *intellectus principiorum* as it enlightens our speculative intellect.[34] In the latter context Thomas mentions *intellectus principiorum* by name and does not, of course, refer to our knowledge of good and evil. Thomas clearly thinks that *synderesis* and *intellectus principiorum* function in exactly similar ways, and he even says so in this section.[35] But by not using the term *synderesis* in the body of the article we are commenting on, he introduces considerable confusion into the discussion of natural law.

Thomas uses the term natural law expansively. The term covers 1) man's condition as subject to eternal law; 2) the principles of the practical intellect which are the parallel to those of the speculative intellect; 3) reason's acknowledgement of our natural tendencies; 4) ordinances of reason which man formulates in accordance with his rational nature. He uses the term, in fact, as the equivalent in the practical intellect of 'truth' in the speculative intellect.

But just as in the case of truth, there is only an analogy between man's moral judgments and divine law. We will see this more clearly if we examine the habit of *synderesis*.

Given that Thomas uses the term natural law so expansively, the question of where *synderesis* ends and ordering practical reasoning begins is of the utmost importance. Granted that all the contents of human reason are only our human mind's analogous grasp of eternal truth, still Thomas thinks that some of our practical knowledge is more certain than others. What then does this sharing in the certainty of the minds of the angels tell us? It may come as a surprise to note that not even the commands of the Decalogue are given us by *synderesis*.[36] It seems absolutely clear that the only moral information we receive from *synderesis* is the first principle: good is to be done and evil is to be avoided. With this principle also comes the spontaneous recognition of the goodness of survival as an individual, as a member of a group and as a rational being.[37] (These latter can be defended as the necessary preconditions of the existence of any given moral agent, but I shall not attempt it here.) This point should not be a controversial one; Thomas' statement that the Decalogue is not included among the first general principles is well known. But in this context the point may indeed need special emphasis.

Human nature is created by God with a special participation in God which is the rational soul. Participation is a term of analogy for Thomas, with far-ranging consequences. In epistemological terms it means that man is given a rational soul which is analogous to the divine mind. This epistemological relation Thomas expresses ontologically as participation. The two abilities of man's rational soul which are analogous to those of God are man's ability to know the truth and to act for an end. It would seem to have been enough for Thomas to simply make these two characteristics part of human nature, but he had at hand in the tradition two terms which he found useful. The first, *intellectus principiorum,* he found in Aristotle; the second, *synderesis,* had been in the medieval tradition at least since Jerome. Moreover, the theory of truth which his adaptation of Aristotle led him to formulate seemed in need of some assurance that the truth which we know and the good which we pursue are the same, although analogously known, as those which are the transcendental true and good. Thus he adds the two habits of *intellectus principiorum* and *synderesis* to the rational soul.

The two have both theological and philosophical importance. Theologically, they are an assurance that man's mind conforms to reality in the way in which the Creator intended. Philosophically they function to provide the mind with what Thomas calls the necessary starting points, first principles, in its knowing the truth and pursuing the good. The two habits generate principles which are underivable and yet necessarily true. The chief of these are, for *intellectus principiorum*: being cannot be affirmed and denied simultaneously; for *synderesis*: good is to be pursued, evil is to be avoided. While Thomas states these as truths about the world which we come to know spontaneously, this statement has the same force as saying that they are truths about the way in which our minds come to know the world. For Thomas the two are the same thing, because of his theological understanding of the ways in which the two habits are God-given for just this purpose. But even this theological assurance is a very limited one, extending only to the first principles themselves, and not to the conclusions which we derive from them.

Thomas once held a very different notion of natural law. The theory expressed in the *Commentary on the Sentences* was based on our knowledge of the natural purpose of specific human actions and Thomas did not explain how we come to know these purposes.[38] Around the time of the writing of *de Veritate* he decided that *synderesis* is the power by which we come to know the precepts of the natural law. Thomas argues that the highest thing in man is something which he has in common with the angels, because there are overlappings in the hierarchy of beings:

> Hence it is that human nature, insofar as it comes in contact with the angelic nature, must both in speculative and practical matters know truth without investigation. And this knowledge must be the principle of all the knowledge which follows, whether speculative or practical, since principles must be more stable and certain. Therefore, this knowledge must be in man naturally, since it is a kind of seed plot containing in germ all the knowledge which follows, and since there preexist in all natures certain natural seeds of the activities and

effects which follow. Furthermore this knowledge must be habitual so that it will be ready for use when needed.

Thus, just as there is a natural habit of the human soul through which it knows principles of the speculative sciences, which we call understanding of principles (*intellectus principiorum*), so, too, there is in the soul a natural habit of first principles of action, which are the universal principles of the natural law. This habit pertains to synderesis.[39]

The text of the previous pages could be read as a commentary on this passage, but several points in it should be singled out. Thomas clearly thinks that the knowledge which is gained as a result of these two habits is "higher" than the knowledge we gain through the use of our ordinary knowing ability. It is also clear that this knowledge, although it is *knowledge,* that is, about the world outside the human mind, is also the form of everything else in the human mind. Thomas' way of putting this is to say that it is the "principle" of all the knowledge which follows. These are things which are true of all that the mind knows, and therefore true of the way in which the mind knows. It could be argued that the chief difference between what Thomas is here saying and certain similar ideas in Kant is that Thomas has a theological assurance that these truths are true of reality and not merely of the mind.[40] While the effect is the same for the two, Thomas does not speak of *a priori*s of the human mind but of *a priori* truths. The difference in terminology has had the most profound results for the understanding of natural law.

A reconstruction of the types of law to include the various elements we have been discussing will yield no surprises at this point but should help to clarify Thomas' terminology:

1) *God's knowledge and will*
Eternal law is the disposition of the universe by God. It differs from the divine ideas formally inasmuch as the latter are known, whereas the former is willed into being.

2) *Things*
Things in this world conform to the divine ideas and are directed by the eternal law. With regard to truth Thomas calls this the truth of things (which I have been calling natural

truth), but with regard to law he makes a distinction. The conformity of human persons to the eternal law Thomas calls natural law; the conformity of the nonpersonal creation he calls by no special name and describes as conforming to the eternal law. Natural law is then, strictly speaking, a conformity of man to the eternal law.

3) *Special knowledge of man*
We come to know this conforming first through *synderesis,* by which we come to know *the first principle of the practical reason,* and secondly, through natural inclination, by which we come to acknowledge precepts of natural law.[41] (Parallelly, *intellectus principiorum* teaches us the first principle of understanding.)

4) *Other knowledge of man, whether of a speculative or a practical kind*
In the speculative intellect Thomas calls this truth of a secondary but proper kind. In the practical intellect Thomas makes a distinction depending whether on the mode of promulgation is by human authority or by reason, and thus refers both to *secondary principles of the natural law* and to *human law.*

Thomas maintains the double-level theory of truth for explicit theological reasons and at the cost of having to face problems like the one presented by natural law. He does not give us, with natural law, the knowledge of the mind of the Creator that he resolutely refuses to give us everywhere else. On the other hand, his awareness of the analogical status of human knowledge did not prevent him from attempting to formulate that knowledge or trying to speak of the human good. (At least not until the very end, if the story of his mystical experience is to be believed.) It may be that these reflections on the imperfect adequacy of human language were something Thomas formulated for abstract theological reasons, but actually attended to hardly at all when 'doing ethics'. Or it may be that he was able to see that, though human beings never have absolute truth, they must do the best they can with what truth they have. In this latter case, Thomas might be the model of the moral philosopher or moral theologian. For historical reasons we are acutely and practically aware of the variability of human moral practice in a way in which Thomas was not. We need a doctrine of analogy for practical reasons.

The Early Theory

Thomas Aquinas died before completing the summary of medieval theology (recast in Aristotelian terms) for which he is justly famous. The *Summa* was, however, complete in outline at his death and, in fact, all that remained of his projected outline was a discussion of some of the seven sacraments. After his death fellow members of the Dominican Order put together a pastiche of Thomas' earlier writing according to his proposed outline. This volume has subsequently become well known as the *Supplementum* to the *Summa Theologiae.*[42] In dealing with the sacrament of marriage, Thomas' confrères and disciples used, among other things, a text which Thomas had written many years before his death as part of his graduate studies at the University of Paris. This early text, published in full as his *Commentum in Quatuor Libros Sententiarum,* contains Thomas' lengthy examination of one of the problem texts for theologians of the Middle Ages: it concerns the polygamy of the patriarchs. An aspiring theologian of the thirteenth century was expected to be able to explain the differences in moral behavior between the many marriages of Abraham, David, Solomon, etc., and the strict monogamy of his own times. Thomas' answer to this conundrum has received a fair amount of attention in our own times where natural law has been invoked to reinforce a sexual morality not much different from that of the thirteenth century. Nevertheless, I think it will be clear that Thomas' earlier understanding of natural law is only barely reconcilable with that of his mature work and, in fact, is so mostly because of a linguistic ambiguity which the later Thomas is willing to exploit. However, I am aware that such a reconciliation has been common in Thomistic studies. A persuasive rejection of this convention of the Thomistic school could, I suppose, be the subject of a book in itself. I shall not try to argue thus persuasively but only review the theory of the early work and explain why I find it very different from that of the *Summa.* The doctrine of the *Summa Theologiae* will be the chief focus of subsequent chapters. It seems to me more in keeping with Thomas' general epistemological position and is also consistent with his teachings on the 'good', *synderesis,* and the law as found in *de Veritate* and the *Summa Contra Gentiles*. (Of course, quite apart from considerations of Thomas Aquinas' consistency, the later theory seems to me to be much more correct.)

In the *Commentum* Thomas uses a distinction between the primary ends of an action and its secondary ends as a basis for his distinction between what he calls, at that time, primary and secondary precepts of natural law. One need only note that he uses this distinction with regard to the ends of marriage to recognize that he is handling, to his own purposes, the celebrated distinction of the 'ends' of marriage developed by St. Augustine. It is the Augustinian designation of procreation of children as the primary end of marriage, and mutual help and the sacrament as secondary, that Thomas uses to explain how the patriarchs were allowed to have more than one wife.

We can understand the dilemma this practice posed for the Middle Ages. In that time both bigamy (not to mention polygamy) and divorce were unheard of. And, yet, in the Bible men otherwise worthy of respect and even veneration were described as following this forbidden practice. The matter must have become even more controversial as medieval Europe came more and more into contact with the Moslem world which had continued to allow a man more than one wife. Thirteenth-century theologians did not have a twentieth-century understanding of cultural change or an explicit understanding of the 'development of doctrine' which nineteenth-century J. H. Newman would become famous for describing. Thomas' solution to what must have seemed a dilemma was to distinguish between two kinds of 'ends' or 'purposes' of marriage. It was to his advantage that this distinction, although not his own way of expressing it, could be traced to the most influential Christian thinker outside the Bible, Augustine of Hippo. In other words, Thomas was able to appeal to an understanding of marriage widely, even universally, accepted in his time. Thus, Thomas is able to use natural law categories in an analysis of the inherent rights or wrongs of a specific action describable strictly in non-moral terms. His aim is to explain the practice of the patriarchs as an allowable dispensation from a universal law. Polygamy, he thinks, does not violate the *primary* end of marriage, the procreation of children, even though it considerably affects the fulfillment of the other purposes. Thus, Thomas argues, it is possible to imagine in appropriate circumstances that a man would be allowed more than one wife because, obviously, it is possible for a man to engender a child of more than one woman. Keeping the same reasoning, Thomas disallows women to have more than one husband because it is impossible for a woman to conceive by more than one man. We should look at Thomas' own words.

In the most relevant passage Thomas begins by saying that all things

> are imbued with certain principles whereby they are enabled . . . to exercise their proper actions proportionate to their end.

He goes on to note that

> Since man, of all animals knows the aspect of the end, and the proportion of the action to the end, it follows that he is imbued with a natural concept, whereby he is directed to act in a befitting manner and this is called the *natural law* or the *natural right,* but in other animals the *natural instinct* . . . Now whatever renders an action improportionate to the end which nature intends to obtain by a certain word is said to be contrary to the natural law. But an action may be improportionate either to the principal or the secondary end and in either case this happens in two ways. First on account of something which wholly hinders the end; . . . secondly on account of something that renders the attainment of the principal or secondary end difficult, or less satisfactory. Accordingly if an action be improportionate to the end, through hindering the principal end directly, it is forbidden by the first precepts of the natural law.
>
> If however, it be in any way improportionate to the secondary end, or again to the principal end, as rendering its attainment difficult or less satisfactory, it is forbidden, not indeed by the first precepts of the natural law but by the second which are derived from the first even as conclusions in speculative matters receive our assent by virtue of self-known principles.[43]

The passage suggests that natural law can be expressed in clear propositional precepts and that such precepts can be ranked according to whether they are essential or not. Primary precepts are the essential ones and they direct us to use a thing or perform an action according to its primary end. They are, therefore, known to us inasmuch as we know the specific and essential purposes of things and actions. Secondary precepts follow from the primary ones. Thus, it would be contrary to the secondary precepts of natural law to make the primary end of an action more difficult or less satisfactory. The distinction and indeed the entire understanding of morality that is sketched here hinges on our ability to know the essential *telos* of human action or of things in the world. It should not surprise us that Thomas is able to be so confident about knowing the purposes of human sexuality. The position he takes would have been incontrovertible and, indeed, almost self-evident in his own time. Even in his later theory he will use the ambiguity of the word 'nature' to allow that that what nature teaches "all animals" ought to be considered as part of natural law. Nevertheless his later theory does go considerably beyond the earlier one in rejecting the notion that the end of actions determines primary precepts of natural law. On the one hand, he will later say that the "good" for humans will determine what is moral and, on the other hand, he will abandon the distinction between primary and secondary precepts altogether. (I am not, of course, suggesting that the good for human beings lies in using things contrary to their natural purposes, if they are known, but only that it is significant that Thomas moves his focus from the nature of things and of describable action onto human nature itself.)

Most important, Thomas does not tell us how we are to find which is the primary and which is the secondary end of an action. The examples he uses, deleted from the text above, are from eating, and his reference to instincts may mean that he is speaking solely of bodily functions of man. At any rate, it is clear that he had no difficulty assigning the primary-secondary distinction to the ends of marriage (although he does argue that *sacramentum* is the most excellent of the marriage goods, even though it is not most essential);[44] the doctrine was too well established in the tradition to cause trouble. With respect to the natural ends of things other than marriage, however, he offers us little help in distinguishing primary from secondary ends. Since Thomas speaks of this distinction only in the context of marriage, we do not know how he would proceed in other matters and the ease with which this distinction can be made with respect to marriage, following Augustine, makes it possible for him to continue to use this analysis of the ends of an action as an example of natural law. Even in the *Summa* itself, although primary and secondary precepts are not used in the context of sins against temperance, he does speak of "unnatural vice." But we have here a notion of natural law very different from that presented in *Secunda Secundae* with regard to the way in which it is known, and it is that later teaching to which we shall return. One important respect in which the two doctrines remain the same, however, is in the mutability of the secondary precepts:

> Since, however, human acts must needs vary according to the various conditioning of persons, times, and other circumstances, the aforesaid conclusions do not proceed from the first precepts of the natural law so as to be binding in all cases, but only in the majority; for such is the entire matter of ethics according to the Philosopher.[45]

Thomas here argues that the patriarchs had received a dispensation from the lawgiver (God) "through an inward inspiration, vouchsafed originally to the holy patriarchs."[46]

In the *Summa,* Thomas does not speak of primary precepts at all, and uses the term secondary precepts only rarely and always in context where he is making a significant distinction between the two kinds of precepts. Instead of primary precepts he refers to "precepts of the natural law" and we shall note that these are not the same as 'natural law.' The difference in terminology between the *Commentum* and the *Summa* seems to be significant because, whereas the earlier terminology made clear that both kinds of precepts prohibit specific actions and that they are similar in knowability and origin, the latter terminology implies a much wider distinction between the precepts of the natural law and the secondary precepts derived from them. Thomas' avoidance of the term primary precept seems deliberate and implies a qualitative distinction which is not present in the *Commentum* where primary and secondary precepts are both referred to.

Thomas seems to have decided around the time when he was

writing *de Veritate* to consider natural law in this new light. It is there that he speaks of the precepts of natural law being the results of *synderesis*. The later *Summa Contra Gentiles* does not mention *synderesis* or natural law, although in the context of that relatively untechnical treatise such a discussion may have been deemed inappropriate. That work does contain a rather simplified version of the same teachings:

> As a result of precepts of divine law, man's mind is subordinated to God, and all other things that are in man's power are ordered under reason. Now, the natural order requires that lower things be subject to higher things. Therefore, the things prescribed by divine law are naturally right in themselves.[47]

Most of all, the difference between natural law in the *Commentum* and in the *Summa* is that in the former natural law is a matter of the *ends of actions* whereas in the latter it is a matter of the *good of man*. That is, in the *Commentum,* Thomas examines a particular action—in this case sexual intercourse—and determines from its end or purpose what the natural law is. We shall see later that it is not particular actions he examines in his later theory but the nature of man and human happiness. Neither formulation is without its difficulties, and we shall have to examine the ways in which Thomas indicates that we come to know the good of man. But the earlier formulation can be reconciled with the latter only on the basis that what reason directs us toward is the good of man and at the same time reason directs us to know the end of an action. But by the time of the writing of the *Summa* Thomas seems far from willing to assert that such knowledge could belong to natural law.

Good and Will

A third point concerning Thomas Aquinas which deserves special attention is related to the two previous ones we have looked at. We have already noted that Thomas distinguishes the practical intellect from the speculative one and thus distinguishes matters of truth from those of goodness. We have also seen that Thomas' later understanding of natural law is considerably different from that of his earliest work. 'Good' is a difficult concept and we shall have to spend the next chapter looking at it in some depth. Here we shall only note some of the peculiarities of Thomas' usage of this term.

The first thing to be said of Thomas' use of the phrase "the practical intellect" is that it indicates an awareness that we would be more likely to describe as the difference between moral language and descriptive language. The medieval categories 'practical intellect' and 'speculative intellect' seem to make that modern distinction, but in a characteristically premodern way. The second thing to be noted is that there is a veil of mystery around the word 'good', a mystery which for Thomas is associated with the human desire for happiness and with the unknowability of God. It is well known that Thomas follows Aristotle in identifying the good, which he describes as "what all men desire," with human happiness. In a lengthy passage in the *Summa Theologiae* he discusses what the happiness of human beings could possibly be and concludes, quite predictably, that the happiness of human beings is God.[48] The difficulty, however, is that human beings do not have an apprehension of God and Thomas argues this both for theological reasons which need not detain us here, and for very practical reasons arising from a common-sense understanding of human beings. For if, Thomas thinks, human beings could apprehend God, there would be no point in discussing moral choice, since humans would not have the ability to not pursue God.

Thomas' doctrine of the will of man is firmly rooted in a more general idea of appetancy, a notion that needs some explanation. Without intending to be anthropomorphic, Thomas explains that things which act in particular ways do so because they have a natural tendency to do so. This insight seems unobjectionable, though circular. "We must observe that some inclination follows every form: for example, fire, by its form, is inclined to rise, and to generate its like."[49] What may strike us as strange about this explanation is that Thomas uses the language of appetite and desire to explain this general 'tendency' of inanimate things to act in a particular way. Although he usually uses the word 'appetite' only in connection with living things, reserving the word 'tendency' to inanimate subjects, he maintains that natural tendencies indicate that things move toward their own perfection. The object of the tendencies of things is the good for that thing, its perfection.

In animals, to whom apprehension is ascribed, natural tendencies exist, but there is also

> an inclination surpassing the natural inclination, which is called the natural appetite. And this superior inclination belongs to the appetitive power of the soul, through which the animal is able to desire what it apprehends, and not only that to which it is inclined by its natural form.[50]

Thomas seems to have in mind here the notion that animals will do certain things—breathe, for example—as a result of a natural tendency (over which it needs no control, and which does not need to be apprehended) but will do others—procreate is one example he uses—as a result of apprehension and thus of natural appetite. It is important to realize that 'apprehend' here means 'apprehend by the senses'.

Finally, there is in man a rational appetite, a tending toward the things that are known by the mind and recognized by the will as good. Man also has a sensitive appetite, like that of the animals, and tendencies which follow from the simple existence of his form. The three appetites seem rather confusing, but they do seem to be a way of speaking about another insight that we would find, in its language at least, more familiar. Whether or not we can easily distinguish what Thomas would call a natural tendency from a natural appetite, we would accept the general principle that we are subject to stimulus-response reactions. This responding in a consistent way to stimuli seems to be what Thomas is calling natural tendencies or appetites. And, in fact, the response of a natural appetite to a specific stimulus is determined, according to Thomas:

> The sensitive power does not compare different things with each other, as reason does: but it simply apprehends one thing. Therefore according to that one thing, it moves the sensitive appetite in a determined way.[51]

The will, however, is not determined. It would be determined if we could apprehend God with our intellect in this life, for he is the proper object of the will, and the will presented with the vision of God has no choice but to choose him. But since in this life nothing is apprehended as universal good, the will is not determined toward anything:

> As the capacity of the will regards the perfect and universal good, its capacity is not subjected to any individual good. And therefore it is not of necessity moved by it.[52]

If what happened when we formed the concept good was that we were apprehending God, then the will would indeed be inclined toward that good, but it would be "inclined" toward it with a necessity that would eliminate all further discussion of morals. There would be no freedom of the will:

> There are some things which have a necessary connection with happiness, by means of which things man adheres to God, in whom alone true happiness consists. Nevertheless, until through the certitude of the Divine Vision the necessity of such connection be shown, the will does not adhere to God of necessity, nor to those things which are of God.[53]

It is precisely because the practical intellect does not apprehend God that man has freedom of choice.

Thomas' point is paradoxical here, and it is a paradox with both theological and epistemological implications. On the one hand we cannot have an apprehension of what true happiness is, because that true happiness is the vision of God. On the other hand, we could not perform any actions intentionally at all unless we have some notion of the end of our actions:

> But an agent does not move except out of intention for an end. For if the agent were not determinate to some particular effect, it would not do one thing rather than another; consequently, in order that it produce a determinate effect, it must, of necessity, be determined to some certain one, which has the nature of an end.[54]

To restate the paradox: on the one hand, only God is, for Thomas, the proper object of human will; on the other hand, we do not have any apprehension of him. It is because we lack a direct knowledge of God that humans have freedom with respect to lesser goods. In a sense, Thomas could resolve the paradox presented by suggesting that the notion of natural law originates here. For if there are some objects which humans always choose as good, it must be because these lesser goods bear some relation to the true good of humans—God. But though it leads in the direction of looking for the constants of human moral behavior, and even suggests in a very theological way an explanation of why there are such constants, we should acknowledge that the paradox remains. There is a mysteriousness about moral activity to which we will return in the last chapter.

THREE

Seeking to Be Good

The preceding two chapters have cleared the ground for the consideration of natural law itself. The first was concerned with stating what a natural law theory ought to contain, even in spite of modern attacks on the notion of natural law. The second was an attempt to clear away the claim that Thomas Aquinas relies on a claim of absolute certainty about what the natural law is. Because of the medieval language of the argument in the previous chapter, the discussion of some of the theological and metaphysical background of Thomas' thinking may have seemed a digression. In the long run, however, the framework Thomas provides for understanding human knowledge—in this case moral knowledge—will be an important historical precedent for claims I consider essential to understanding morality and natural law. In this chapter we begin our discussion of matters obviously related to questions usually associated with natural law and, indeed, with ethics in general.

Specifically, we are here concerned with the origins of the sense of morality. We are asking the question "Why are human beings moral?" By implication, also, we are dealing with a whole range of fundamental questions about the nature of morality. But such questions are notoriously difficult and, in fact, they may be insoluble. An enormous amount of energy has gone into attempts to make clear what morality means and it may be that the confusion that still reigns on the subject is the most we can hope for. Nevertheless, a retreat too quickly into the category of mystery would be too easy and not do justice to the apparently unquenchable human desire to understand.

So where might we begin? The usual starting point of natural law theories such as the one set out by Thomas is also our choice, but it is a starting point that has hardly been immune to criticism. In fact, the chief difficulty many might have in understanding an ethical theory constructed along the lines of that set out by Thomas would probably be his troublesome starting point.

This is, of course, his insistence that human beings naturally desire to be good and that this ordinary desire is an adequate explanation of the origins of morality. There are two assertions here, and both are problematic. The first is that the desire to be good is an ordinary, indeed necessary, human experience. The second is that this desire is an adequate explanation of morality. Of the two, the first is the less troublesome, but both require discussion and elaboration.

Thomas' discussion of this starting point is quite short: it is 'good' that first enters our apprehension when we are bent on doing something, and thus, for the practical intellect the starting point is "good is to be done and evil is to be avoided."[1] So brief is Thomas' discussion of this point, and so often discussed, that it seems worthwhile here to avoid his language and to look at the idea of a human desire for goodness in a different way. At one time the assertion of a basic human desire for goodness might have seemed self-evident—Thomas seems to have thought so. But in our time, in the latter half of what someone has called our worst century yet, a century filled with genocide, wars and pogroms, with atom bombs and napalm, it may seem almost disgusting to say that humans fundamentally desire to be good (have an "appetite" for the good of their nature, Thomas says). But the thirteenth century was not without its own moral outrages, calamities and shortfalls. If the assertion made sense to Thomas, it could hardly have been because he was living in a time of moral perfection, a perfection from which we have since fallen. Nevertheless, Thomas makes the assertion and he does so, I think, for good reason. Still, moral evil exists, and it is a fundamental problem for any theory of the naturalness of morality. How can we explain what appears to be an enormous overestimation of human beings?

One way of doing so would be to reassert the traditional doctrine that human beings are sinful and that this sinfulness affects both our intellects and our wills. That is, because of sin we sometimes fail to know what is really good, and sometimes, even though we know better, we fail to act in pursuit of the good. In some form or another—one need not use the Christian word sin—such an assertion seems incontestable.

The assertion of human sinfulness can be taken too far, however; it can be taken to be a denial of a basic desire to be good at all. Such a denial can be made for the kind of common-sense reasons already mentioned, or for more philosophical ones or out of theological conviction. The theological reasons we shall not deal with here, as they would take us too far afield.[2] The philosophical objections will be answered, indirectly at least, by the rest of this chapter. For the moment it should be noticed that to acknowledge the existence of sin is not automatically to agree that it is the total explanation of human motivation. It is rather to acknowledge that one valid explanation of the difficulty of saying that human beings desire to be good is to stress that the problems involved in human morality are probably not going to be removed by thinking about them. A full theory of morality would have to dwell much longer on this topic than we shall be doing here. It is worth noting, however, that human sinfulness is not being denied. In fact, some of what follows may help to explain it.

A Non-Moral Sense of Good

In spite of the problems associated with human sinfulness, we turn now to the central issue of this chapter. It is essential to the natural law tradition that morality is natural to human beings, that is, that ordinary humans have some sense of what morality requires and that we want to be moral. It is certainly the case that the kind of language we are calling 'moral language' is a cultural universal. It is also the case that the ability to understand moral language presupposes the sense of morality I am calling essential to the natural law tradition. But although the thesis that morality is natural to humans may seem unexceptionable, it has proved uncommonly difficult to elucidate. The literature abounds with alternative attempts to explain the sources of morality or the "meaning" of moral language and none seems capable of winning universal acceptance. Perhaps it would be enough to simply appeal to the universality of moral language as adequate justification of the thesis that morality is natural to humans and to proceed to another issue. We could then leave it to the social scientist to struggle to explain to us *why* morality is universal. Such a procedure seems unsatisfactory for two reasons. The first is that too much of the argument of this book hangs on the presupposition of the normality of morality to pass it by so easily. The second is that the line between naturalism and morality has been drawn so sharply in this century, beginning with Moore, that any naturalistic explanation of morality is too easily dismissed as involving a 'non-moral' sense of good. The remainder of this chapter is an attempt to redescribe the relationship between naturalism and morality in such a way as to make the two compatible, but not identical, while at the same time shedding some light on the assertion that humans naturally desire goodness.

A beginning point that can help us past the difficulty of imagining that persons ordinarily desire to be good might be to consider 'good' in a psychological or non-moral sense. In our times we ordinarily distinguish between those judgments we call 'prudential' which we can loosely define as being based on self-interest, and those which take into account the interests of others and of larger and larger communities. We use for the latter judgments the word 'moral'. The distinction is not as clear as it is sometimes taken to be, and to this we shall return. At any rate, moral judgments in this latter sense have caused the greatest difficulty in the description of the workings of ordinary human language. An adequate characterization of how we use the word 'good' in this moral context has been debated for most of this century, at least, and it has proven to be a difficult task. For the moment, let us limit ourselves to looking at the word 'good' in a non-moral, prudential sense.

When talking about human motivation, any interpretation almost automatically invites evaluation by the modern discipline of psychology and such other modern methods of investigating human nature as sociology and anthropology. (Indeed, all of these have sometimes seemed all too eager to explain the 'ultimate' source of human behavior.) One place where their concern has been of interest to the moralist has been the issue of psychological egoism. This latter is not simply the contention that where humans do something freely, they do it because they want to do it. Such an assertion is analytically true and uncontroversial. Psychological egoism is usually identified with a more troublesome proposal, that whatever human beings want to do they want to do it because it is perceived to be in the self-interest of the agent to do so. In this form the claims of psychological egoism are frequently thought to be inimical to morality, which in its most specific sense is usually thought to involve a modicum of altruism. What the claim of psychological egoism does is reduce all human behavior to the self-regarding or prudential level.[3]

There are, however, ways of stating the claims of psychological egoism which are less drastic in their consequences. One such version of psychological egoism which allows room for the possibility of morality is the suggestion that the paramount self-interest of the agent is in maintaining his or her self-esteem or self-respect. This is a less simplistic form of self-interest than some which have been put forward. It does not, for example, identify self-interest with the satisfaction of physical desires for pleasure. Rather it addresses the concerns of an agent on a somewhat broader scale. One of the ways in which this broader scale is evident is that it emphasizes the human need to make sense of the one life each of us has apparently been given. In the face of this obvious limitation, self-respect means the ability to think that one has used one's opportunities well, that one has been 'good', at least in the sense that one has not wasted the one life which we are sure we have.

This minimal sense of good as a psychological necessity is not sufficient to explain morality, but it nevertheless bears examination because, it seems to me, it permits the possibility of both naturalistic reasons for action and moral ones. At the outset it is the naturalistic reason that is most obvious. At this point in our discussion we are using the word 'good' in the non-moral sense of maintaining one's self-respect, of thinking well of oneself. And one important element of this self-esteem maintenance is our awareness that we are not immortal.

A fundamental human experience seems to be that connected with time and death.[4] We have learned over and over again that opportunities presented by this particular moment will not be repeated. We have also learned that the number of opportunities offered to us is predictably limited, that we are finite, that we will die. Finitude and mortality are commonly thought of as depressing topics and yet it seems no exaggeration to say that a perception of these topics conditions, however subtly, almost all of our ordinary consciousness. The ordinary process of living a human life is inevitably colored by our perception that we have moment by moment only one life to live and that neither the moment nor, in the long run, the life appear to be repeatable. Always and everywhere we seem to be bounded by finiteness and death. More than anything else it is the perception of finiteness which creates the urgency behind the human desire to be good. For being good means ultimately that one is able to justify the way in which he or she has spent the moments which add up to an unrepeatable human life.

It might be argued that there is no need to look any further for the origins of human moral language than the basic unrepeatability of human experience. Since I will not have this moment again, since I will not have this particular life again, how shall I use it? Of the various choices available to me at this moment, what shall I do? It is obvious, of course, that this kind of question cannot be answered in an abstract way. It is equally obvious that in answering such questions, I must pay attention to the circumstances of my life, and yet that, in spite of the circumstances, I must make choices which cannot be entirely explained by the facts of the matter.

One basis of the origin of morality, and especially of some of its urgency, lies in the need of human beings to make sense of their own lives. I have not yet attempted to be more specific about what it means to make sense of one's life. The process can be analyzed—at least in part—but at the level of the individual that task can be relegated to psychology. Ernest Becker compares the development of psychological technique for analyzing the processes of maintaining "self-esteem" to the Darwinian doctrine of natural selection.[5] The latter brings a cogent explanation to the diversity and similarity in nature which has been long observed, while self-esteem gives us the unique explanation of human diversity and similarity. He notes, summarizing a wealth of material: "The whole early training period of the child can be understood in one simple way: it is the period in which he learns to maintain his self-esteem in more-or-less constant fashion by adapting his reactions to the dictates and the possibilities of his human environment" (SE, p. 328). Psychologists disagree, of course, on much of how this process is to be explained. But Becker's generalization would seem to be sound and we can safely leave precise explanation of the process to the psychologists. On the other hand, of course, psychologists can only offer an explanation of human behavior in a general sort of way unless they engage in hours of face-to-face conversation with a given individual and then their explanations may be of value only to that individual.

Not wanting to be caught in a crossfire of psychological theories, let us use the term in a common sense kind of way until we return to it at the end of the next chapter. The life of a human being is complicated in the extreme and we must all respond to a wide variety of sometimes irreconcilable demands made on us by our status in the world. Such are, for example, the demands for our own survival, for a modicum of security, both physical and psychic, for taking our place in an ever-widening circle of communities which sometimes place conflicting demands upon us, for truth and consistency. It is out of the conflict of these calls upon us and our own need to feel that we are making sense of our lives that humans fashion morality in the widest sense.[6] We are locating the beginnings of morality here because it is only by doing so that one is able to do justice to the morality of the artist who pursues beauty and that of the thinker who pursues truth as well as that of the doer who pursues goodness. All of us are probably moved by all three of these concerns and it is by one or another or all three of these concerns that we attempt to make sense of our lives. It is because individuals are so motivated that morality is built into human languages. All of us, of course, are born into a language about the world and our first understandings of how to make sense of our lives—in other words of how to use the word 'good'—come to us from the communities into which we are born. The process of learning to use that word ('good') independently is undoubtedly a long and complicated one. (In fact one can well ask how many of us ever learn to do so with complete independence.)[7] It is not the purpose of this argument to try to analyze what human beings are like uninfluenced by their languages, but rather to question the relationship between moral language and reality as we can know it.

Clearly individuals as well as communities will make moral judgments differently depending upon a variety of factors: their history, their external circumstances, their standards of consistency, their often only implicit understandings of what it means to be a human being, etc. What makes sense to an educated person in the late twentieth century may be quite different from what made sense to a soldier in the early Roman Empire, and clearly some of these differences can be explained relatively easily by looking at the circumstances of the lives of the two agents. A maidservant in Victorian England probably made sense of her life in a way obviously different from a princess of the Nile. As we learn more about human beings from such sciences as psychology and sociology, we can expect to better understand the ways in which the process of making sense of one's life is conditioned by the circumstances of the life one happens to be living. And as this is true of individuals, so it appears to be true also of communities of varying sizes: the family, the neighborhood, the state, as well as in varying times and places. Nothing in this study is intended to deny these relativities; rather, the contention is that such changes have in common a basic human need to feel good about ourselves and that there are some constants which show up despite the differences in patterns which we choose to help us fulfill this need.

Speaking descriptively of the motivation of the subject, we have been using the phrase 'make sense of our lives' or even 'feel good about ourselves'. We should note that these expressions do not contain enough of an awareness of the givenness of the world around us. Although we may experience the moral drive as the need to feel good about ourselves, a more profound understanding of this drive—and in fact the only one which explains its urgency for at least some of us—is to say that our ability to feel good about ourselves is dependent upon our situation in the world. This is to say that although the expression '*feeling* good about ourselves' may be more intelligible to us in a common-sense kind of way, the basic desire of human beings is in fact to *be* good. When we feel good about ourselves, we feel that we *are,* in fact, good, and that this goodness is not simply our own personal judgment, but rather true in terms of the realities of our situation. Earlier we spoke of the sinfulness of humans and here we should at least be aware that our problem is not simply an intellectual one. The gap between actually *being* good and *feeling* good about ourselves can be an enormous one. As such, the possible disparity is a problem not simply of our language systems, but also of our personal histories. Not only do both communities and individuals make mistakes about what it actually means to be good, but also both communities and individuals seem able to feel good about doing what, in some sense, they have already decided they ought not to feel good about. The point here is that in saying that human beings desire to be good, we must both affirm that such a statement is literally true and yet admit that we affirm this even in the face of the all-too-obvious evils that we humans have done and continue to do. The Nazi leader giving the order for mass slaughter may be trying to satisfy his desire to make sense of his life as much as the hermit in the desert or the housewife making dinner for her husband.

The double focus of the human need to maintain self-esteem is then: first, that humans need to make sense of their lives, especially given the fact of mortality, and second, that such a sense of self-esteem must be achieved within the framework of a given historical situation. Whatever else one may say of the first of these, and I shall say more later, the fact of inevitable death can stand as a symbol for all that gives urgency to the quest for self-respect or self-esteem. With regard to the second, it is only because humans respond in somewhat predictable ways to circumstances that we can have any "science" of human behavior at all—be it psychology, sociology, or whatever. It is because the two must be combined that self-respect is a good place to establish a naturalistic base for understanding the moral dimension of human life. But before we proceed with our discussion of morality, one possible objection must be dealt with. It is the objection that human morality can be understood solely in terms of conditioning, that is, in terms of the human sciences we have just mentioned.

Of course we have been taught how to live our lives by our parents, our peers and others, and there are times when the word 'good' seems to mean only what those others have taught us. In spite of what we have already said about the need for self-respect, we can occasionally make sense of the question "Why should I be good?" We can do so because good has been defined according to a standard which can be discovered to be that of one's parents or peer group, or some other community to which we belong. That is to say that sometimes we find ourselves making judgments about other people and even ourselves in terms of what other people have expected us to believe. Finding such obvious origins for some of our moral standards and also finding that some of these standards can vary from place to place or from time to time has lead some people to conclude that all human moral judgments are nothing but the result of cultural conditioning. It is necessary here to state a disclaimer. Although the main thrust of this study is to talk of the ways in which groups of persons must formulate standards about what it means to be a good human being, we must reject some of the emphasis that has been placed on the notion of the communal basis of morality. While it is true that groups of persons must formulate standards about what it means to be a good human being, the need to think of oneself as good cannot be explained simply in terms of such communal standards. Quite apart from what we have learned from our parents, our peers and so forth about what makes a good human being (and even if we have learned to recognize such influences from other people), we are still faced with the necessity of making sense of our own lives. Rejecting the standards of our parents and our peers does not lift from us the burden of deciding how to live this particular life, and we must inevitably decide how to do so according to what seems best to us. Inevitably, in other words, we must reinvent the meaning of the word 'good'. Inevitably also, reflection reminds us that the meaning of the word is an inevitable consequence of the combination of the facts of our lives and our reflection upon those facts.

I hope it is clear that I am not trying to import into this analysis of the origins of the word 'good' any kind of intuition or any kind of 'non-natural' content for the word. I will indeed later say that in trying to make sense of their lives and of living in the world, human beings will inevitably pursue some moral or non-natural meaning of what it means to be a good human being. To explain such notions it will be necessary eventually to use language which points toward intuition or affectivity or conative knowledge—or simply mystery. But the essential urgency of the human desire for goodness need not be explained by any such special knowledge. It is compatible with most of the formulation of natural law that follows to assert that what humans have come to call 'good' has been arrived at only as a result of a process of trial and error and that the public evaluative sense of 'good' is roughly the equivalent of 'what works', and especially 'what has worked in the past'. This would mean simply that there is an empirical or naturalistic basis for the meaning of 'good' and this is, in fact, one of the theses which we are trying to defend. We must go further, but let us first look at this meaning.

This minimum meaning of the word 'good' would be the result of generations of persons trying to make sense of their lives as limited beings. Individuals and groups give public meaning to the word 'good' by using it to indicate conduct and attitudes which their experience has taught them is conducive to a sense of well-being, inasmuch as it satisfies the needs of persons living in the world. Such uses of the word 'good'—or of other words which commend, etc.—are incorporated into language and passed on to the next generation.[8] It must be a truism that persons do not deliberately teach their children nonsense. There is certainly a *prima facie* case for saying that an established use of the word 'good', one that has survived centuries and been handed down for generations, must have an observably beneficial result. We shall return to this in the next chapter.

There is a certain coherence achieved by grounding morality in the need to maintain self-esteem in this way and by noticing that such a grounding explains a great deal of the development of moral practices and customs. But there are several drawbacks to such a position and these indicate that it is necessary to go further than the naturalism we have been describing. For one thing, the position so far sketched implies a kind of conservatism in which the past is given too weighty an influence in the present. Like such defenders of naturalism as Philippa Foot, I think that attitudes and actions that have been commended for a long time are those to which we ordinarily give the word 'good', though I am not sure she would phrase it this way. But, in my phrasing at least, the past is given a kind of normative quality. It seems as though the usages of the past are almost *verified* through experience, and the burden of proof is on those who would introduce change. While such a conservation may have a legitimate place in natural law theories, another element of such theories is to provide the possibility of providing leverage against a given order of things. Martin Luther King, Jr. was able to cite Thomas Aquinas as one theorist who had provided him with a rationale for trying to change the segregationist order in Birmingham, Alabama.[9] This element of natural law theories is missing in what we have so far said. Secondly, when we speak of an individual's need to make sense of his or her own life we must acknowledge that the urgency of this need can find expression in a variety of decisions about how one should live one's life. Are all such options to be regarded as moral? Is 'good' to be identified in this trivial way as relative to the choices of individual persons? The vast variety of such identifications may never have been clearer than it is today to those who are able to take advantage of our enormous storehouse of information about the past and about other cultures and "lifestyles." Earlier I said that this section would be concerned in the talking about good in a prudential or non-moral sense. What we have said so far does, in fact, seem to be about the psychology of human beings rather than about morality. It has been argued recently that any particular human decision on how one should live one's life can be counted as a morality—that is, as moral for that person—if it is accompanied by certain logical moves; for example the assertion or belief that everyone ought to live in this particular way. There is something correct about this. At least in the short run one ought not to be too prescriptive in defining the meaning of good, especially for individuals.[10] But in general, of course, such a usage makes hopeless any attempt to say that moral reasoning is in touch with reality. All of which tells us that it may be somewhat reductionistic to talk of the origins of morality in terms only of the human dilemma of making sense of life as we can analyze it. But we can go further.

One final objection to remaining content with a notion of 'good' that limits our use of it to what has proved workable in the past is in order. It is one thing to say that our knowledge of good is limited to a matter of trial and error. But such an affirmation begs an important question. It is true that human moral codes show an observable similarity and that it is frequently possible to correlate these similarities with features of the empirical world. What is less easily correlated with the material world in which we live is the existence of moral codes at all—where 'moral' now means having a certain kind of motivation or being concerned with becoming or remaining a certain kind of human being. The resistance of those who understand morality in this way to reducing it to empirical causes is well known and it is here that we can see why their resistance is justified. When we think of a person as acting morally, we are usually doing more than describing their actions. We are also making a judgment about why they are acting—that they are doing something not merely because it promotes their self-interest or survival or for some other empirical motive. They are judged to be doing it because it is good or right. It is because this judgment that to do something is good cannot be exhaustively explained in terms of any natural property, that those who protest against the 'naturalistic fallacy' are reluctant to speak of the relationship between morality and reality. To do so, to talk of a reality that grounds a sense of moral purpose, narrowly defined, in the real world is not to talk of this or that observable datum but rather to talk of a more nebulous sense of reality, one that inevitably strains our empirical categories.

Beyond Naturalism

The self-esteem that humans need, the sense of feeling good about oneself, does not seem to be something humans can confer upon themselves.[11] We have earlier argued that it can only come of a sense that one has lived one's life well, and that it arises out of the historical situation of the person. Although one cannot confer being worthy of esteem upon oneself, there is a need to believe that such worthiness is real, that it is based upon reality. It is here that we find the opening between a merely naturalistic and a moral sense of good. What else does it mean to be worthy of respect than that one is a good human being? And what *is* a good human being? It is worth examining this question.

There is something irreducible about human life: we are constantly confronted with its mysteriousness. It is less popular these days to talk of human motivation as being 'drawn' than of being 'driven' and yet there seems to be something essentially true about both of these metaphors. We have been talking of the driven human sense of needing to make sense of one's life, especially in the face of death, and we are used to a vocabulary which talks about 'human desires'. We are less comfortable with thinking of ourselves as drawn, as having goals or ideals that cannot simply be explained in terms of the immanent needs or wants of our own choosing. And yet important thinkers have frequently spoken of a human desire to become a certain kind of being, as though that desire were not of our own choosing, but rather inherent in being a human being. Speaking of the mystery of human motivation Soren Kierkegaard thought that human beings ultimately desire to become an individual human person in the presence of God.[12] Paul Tillich thought that all human persons have an urgent necessity to become "a person in a community of persons."[13] Thomas Aquinas' way of saying somewhat the same thing was to say that human beings have a "natural drive" "toward those things which lead us to know about God and to live in community."[14] The differences among these three thinkers are perhaps clear enough. Kierkegaard seems to stress more than the others the need to become an individual, an emphasis which Thomas lacks, while Paul Tillich mentions God not at all. But since we are at the moment emphasizing the mystery of human action it is worth dwelling on their similarities. We might say that the dilemma of the human condition is how to be a worthwhile human person and that becoming a person is always a matter of a relationship to at least one other person. The phrase "becoming a person" appears in both Kierkegaard's and Tillich's appropriation. Thomas speaks of the need to know about God; all three talk of other persons, but for Kierkegaard, interestingly, the reference is solely to God. The difference between Kierkegaard and Aquinas might be reducible to the differences between a thirteenth- and a nineteenth-century thinker; but it is possible that we are confronting here a difference more fundamental in what it means to be a good human being.

There is no point dwelling upon the mystery of human conduct at too great a length. For those who are not used to the concept of mystery the ultimate appeal may be to ask them to examine their own conduct and motivation and to reflect upon whatever brings urgency to their own lives, whether it is called rationality, consistency, public accountability, or some other phrase to which they respond. In Bellow's novel of that name, Henderson the Rain King is described as wandering around the world with a heart that kept screaming, "I want, I want" without knowing what it is it wanted. Such a notion, of blind human urgency, seems easier for us to accept than the idea that this urgency is met by an equal urgency from the world around us, that what it means to be a human being is not entirely ours to decide. Of course, we know that we share the world with other persons and that their existence affects ours in incalculable ways. The world in which we must try to maintain our self-esteem is this shared world, even though we would sometimes like to think that our self-esteem was simply a matter of our own choosing, that we could confer goodness on ourselves.

Thomas and Kierkegaard and Tillich can hardly be dismissed as superficial or trivial observers of what it means to be human. Still, we are not likely to be comfortable with a notion of an inner drive to be human in a specific way. This sounds too much like the old Platonic notion of natures or forms or perhaps a mechanistic understanding of natural inclinations, or even a kind of intuition. None of those vocabularies—natures or inclinations or intuitions—seems easy for a modern person to be comfortable with. Because these ways of talking have been around for a long time, yet seem to have little persuasive power, some new attempt to clarify this matter seems to be appropriate. The following is a 'thought experiment'—an attempt to talk about the roots of the human moral experience in a way that makes it more understandable. It is compatible, I think, with the three thinkers just mentioned, as well as with many other thinkers of the past. It is also compatible with presuppositions which might inform the researches of social scientists in several disciplines. But it is not intended to be more than an imaginative aid. The truth or falsity of the suggestion is probably beyond our testing and too great an attention to those questions is not the purpose of presenting this sketch.

Not that the suggestion is new. What if, in spite of the depredations of cultural and personal conditioning, in spite of the distance between the way we are now and the way we should be, we remain somehow, indistinctly in touch with what it would mean to be unsinful, unalienated, full human beings, fully ourselves? What if this possibility lay always somewhere under the surface of any direct consciousness, something we could never really experience in itself, but only as a dim reverberation, an echo, a trace? Such an intimation would not be an intuition in some sense of a Platonic illumination. Our minds would be too confused by the categories of a perceptual scheme that are too removed from reality to be able to compass it. Our minds are shaped by necessities of survival and emotion and need, and not only by these in general, but in particular *forms* all of which are contributors to the degeneration of our ability to perceive reality. Some of these are far worse than others, some of them create conditions in which it is all but impossible for any but the merest handful of individuals to have any inkling of the reality obscured by the categories of what *seems* to be the world.[15]

Such a possibility involves a number of presuppositions. The first of these is perhaps the most obvious: the way we perceive the world is a cultural construct.[16] At its simplest, this means simply that we see the world differently if we are born into an ordinary middle-class American environment than if we are born into an environment of great need in a black ghetto or a poor-white pocket of the Appalachians. We see the world differently if we are born into the mechanized mid-twentieth century than had we been born in a neolithic tribe, or the Roman Empire, or T'ang dynasty China. In this sense, the supposition seems commonsensical. All of these possibilities, if we enter imaginatively into them, strike us as at least partially different from our own world. Surely a world without aspirin and novocaine and x-ray resetting of broken bones would be at least more painful than the one we know now. Still, though we know we cannot hear footsteps fifty feet away or smell animals in the wind, we can adjust the fine tuner of a stereo or a carburetor and we are inclined to think that we are not missing anything in the external world that is of vital importance to us. Nevertheless, we are aware that we know at best only a portion of what it means to be a human being.

If we think of reality not simply as rocks or chairs or as objects in the world, but as the characteristics of human beings, we may be less likely to concede the differences our conditioning gives us. Our own experience of humanness may strike us as full and complete, and we are likely to be willing to judge others according to our own experience. It is difficult to accept that our own experience may be limited or distorted and if we can afford to do so we may respond to such an insight by seeking therapeutic or psychiatric help. We may be inclined to resist the notion that we are obliged to live out the "ordinary miseries of living" as Freud called normality. Not only we ourselves, but past generations have been inclined to this self-satisfied perspective. Especially in some natural law theories we find the assertion that some custom or other is timeless and universal, that it would be the unanimous decision of those who are wise. Sometimes the assertion is put in the mouth of divinity and the custom becomes the will of God or of the gods. And of many such practices—feudal hierarchies, the subjugation of women, the relegation of certain races to inferiority, for examples—we find it hard to understand why anyone put up with them, much less why the wise would agree to them. But if we react to such examples with complacency, thinking that we are beyond such foolishness, we may well wonder what other generations would make of our environmental pollution, our wastefulness, our addiction to drugs. To the social nature of our perceptions of reality we will return later. The essential point for the time being is that we are not seeing reality 'as it is' but rather our vision of it is filtered through the contingencies of our time and our space.

Further, of course, each of us, as well as every human culture, is racked with inconsistencies and is twisted an enormous distance from reality, from a full humanity that would be able to live constantly at its best. We are inclined, perhaps, to identify the causes of this shortfall with sexual tension (the Oedipus complex of the orthodox Freudians) or with the alienation of labor, and these are real sources of human limitation. Or we might consider the source of the problem to be as Kierkegaard thought: the human condition itself, which causes us to construct around ourselves shields which keep us in touch with, at best, only as much reality as we can handle. But whether one talks of psychological conditioning or of social alienation or of sin, the gulf that separates us from unacculturated truth remains. We may speak of 'more' or 'less' but the situation remains a general one. Belaboring the fact that we know only part of reality will not make it palatable, and the difficulty of accepting it is one of the consequences of the second, and more important, presupposition.

This presupposition is the following. In spite of the conditionedness of our perceptions, what it really might be like to be a full human being, reality itself remains an elusive possibility for us. Such a possibility might be explained as an intuition, but that word is associated with a special intellectual illumination and I find it confusing. If intuition is taken as a sense that some actions are more satisfying than others, however, a sense of fitness perhaps analogous to the aesthetic sense, it is usable. The analogy of aesthetics is appropriate here. The sense of balance, proportion,[17] harmony that is associated with painting a pleasing picture, or even decorating a room, can be achieved by using rules already decided upon. One may have decided, for example not to mix certain colors or not to leave too much space blank. Still, behind the rules, and acting as source of the rules and judge of them, is a sense that is perhaps not satisfied or even acknowledged except in the doing of a particular thing. Likewise a sense of moral appropriateness may be formulated in intellectual rules or principles, but the sense that lies behind them is not the same as the principles themselves.

This word picture may be imaginative but it is not as fanciful, or original, as might be supposed. Modern psychological theories have given us a new way of imagining a subconscious world of human drives, and the later Freud was openly mythical when he suggested the existence of a conflict between a life instinct and a death instinct in individuals and society. A reader of the past few paragraphs may see a considerable influence of the Freudian model of the psyche there. But it is worthwhile to note that the word picture might not have seemed so strange to Thomas Aquinas.

As noted in Chapter Two, Thomas believed that the origin of moral language was mysterious and, as a starting point it could not be verified by subsequent reflection. For him the first precept of practical reason, like that of speculative reason, is the certain place where humans share the knowledge of the angels. All of our other knowledge is to be explained by reflection upon our experience. But in reflecting upon ourselves we notice that we are inevitably drawn to seek certain goods, toward which we have "natural inclinations." It is thus that Thomas is able to say that the good is what all desire and to mean by that not simply that what people desire they come to call good but also that what people really desire is the true good. Thomas' vocabulary may grate on the modern ear; we are not accustomed any more to think in terms of angelic knowledge or of natural inclinations, and this verbal difficulty is what my word picture was intended to overcome. Where Thomas speaks of human beings as ordered by God and ordained toward

Him (in spite of our capacity for ignorance and wickedness) I prefer to talk about a *marginal* capacity to experience the world as full human beings—or a marginal capacity to fully experience the world. The claim is not, after all, that humans are always good or always right but that most of us are sometimes aware of what is good and sometimes do the right and that this is apparent in the long run.

Thomas was certainly not unaware of the wide gap between ordinary human choices and reality. In fact, as we saw in Chapter Two, he makes the gap almost impossibly wide. In his terms the true object of the will, the true good, is God Himself, and because this true "end" does not appear in the information available to our senses our will is subsequently free. Nevertheless, of course, the claim is made that there is some valid connection between the goods we choose and our true good—and this again is observable in the long run.

These assertions about the "long run" alert us to another caution about the vocabulary of Thomas Aquinas. His language of "natural inclinations" can be appropriated by such non-cognitivists as Frankena.[18] When he speaks of first principles, however, Thomas sounds much like an intuitionist. If intuition is taken to mean 'a sense of right and wrong' in a vague sense, such a reading can be justified by texts in Thomas. But Thomas should not be thought of assuming that the "first" of first principles means that literally the first thought to enter a child's head is 'good'. I think a strong case can be made for saying that the first associations a child might make with that word is with very elemental desires, but the organized ways in which a child is taught how to use the word good are a much more complicated affair, and are embedded in a whole moral code and to such codes we turn in the next chapter.

FOUR

Reason and Natural Law

One important element which identifies theories of morality as being in the tradition of natural law is the assertion that a sense of morality, in its restricted sense, is part of the ordinary experience of humans. A second is that the requirements of morality can be known through the use of reason. A third is the theological element which asserts that what God requires of us is that we act in accordance with our human moral reasons, that is, in accordance with the natural law. In the previous chapter we examined the first of these elements, suggesting a model of human motivation which is capable of both naturalistic and moral interpretations. In this chapter we shall move on to the second element, that of rationality and in the following one we shall look at *some* of the consequences of our examination for the third of these. A number of modern commentators on natural law, especially Catholics, have stressed that the essential element of the natural law tradition is the first of these, the naturalness of morality. They argue that a necessary precondition for human beings' ability to respond to God's call to live as a member of His people is that we understand the demands of morality in the first place.[1] There is among these commentators less of a tendency to go further, to discuss the relationship between moral codes and natural law. Rightly, the assertion is made that the kind of cataloging of the 'laws' of morality that used to characterize the handbooks of moral theology [2] can no longer be defended, but little or no attempt is made to understand the kind of thinking that made the handbooks useful for so long a time. In this chapter we shall not try to remedy that omission directly. Instead we shall look at the groundwork which underlies both the teachings of the handbooks and the kind of thinking that would replace those teachings with something else. Despite the excesses of the handbooks, which often contained 'objective' judgments on the minutest detail of actions, public moral codes are important and necessary. Their relationship to 'objectivity' is in need of clarification and the remainder of this chapter will address this need.

Neither a commitment to objectivity nor even an espousal of the natural law tradition leads inevitably to the issue of moral codes, the line of thought we will be pursuing. Examples of those who espouse each of these without an interest in moral codes are not difficult to find. William K. Frankena, for example, is committed to the idea of the reality of morality—a position he calls 'ethical absolutism'—but he has never, to my knowledge, associated himself with the natural law tradition or pursued the question of the formation of moral codes.[3] Closer to the language of natural law is the option of developing the basic human desire for goodness in the direction of human virtue. Such a line of thought is one Thomas himself uses extensively, even preferentially, in talking about morals. Recently Stanley Hauerwas has argued that such a way of understanding natural law provides a better understanding of the relationship of ordinary morality to Christian morality than does the emphasis upon moral codes which I shall be pursuing.[4] Hauerwas interprets natural morality "as involving a cluster of roles and relations that an agent must order to have a character appropriate to the limits and possibilities of our existence" (p. 1). This emphasis on "roles and relations" leads him to speak subsequently of virtues, such as honesty and faithfulness.[5]

Drawing out such a relationship between natural law and virtue is valid; emphasis upon rules or codes by no means exhausts the meaning of natural law. But emphasis upon virtue is more appropriate to talking about the morality of an individual than to that of communities and it is the latter which is the chief interest of this study. It is my hope that the analysis that follows will illuminate the ways in which morality is institutionalized, including ways other than Thomas describes in the "Treatise on Law."

H. L. A. Hart

Perhaps the most famous modern attempt to pursue the idea of natural law in the direction we wish to follow is that of H. L. A. Hart. A professor of jurisprudence at Oxford, Hart has defended a "minimal content of natural law" in an influential section of his wide-ranging book, *The Concept of Law*.[6] In the long run, we will wish to move beyond some of the limitations of Hart's analysis, but he is a convenient starting point for a discussion of the content of natural law, beyond the human desire to be good.

By way of preamble, Hart notes:

> Reflection on some very obvious generalizations—indeed truisms—concerning human nature and the world in which men live, shows that as long as these hold good, there are certain rules of conduct which any social organization must contain if it is to be viable . . . [But] With them are found, both in law and morals, much that is peculiar to a particular society and much that may seem arbitrary or a mere matter of choice.[7]

Thus, implicit in Hart's description of a "minimal content of natural law" is the point of view that he is talking about universal patterns of human mores. He is speaking not of individuals but of systems of laws, although his position as regards the individual and his motivation is considerably different from that found in more familiar theories. Hart "attenuates" natural law first of all by reducing it to the basic human need for survival. In other words, where Thomas sees a number of basic inclinations—and to this we shall return—Hart finds only one:

> The actions which we speak of as those which are naturally good to do, are those which are required for survival; the notions of a human need, or harm, and of the *function* of bodily organs or changes rests on the same simple fact. Certainly if we stop here, we shall have only a very attenuated version of natural law: for the classical exponents of this outlook conceived of survival (*perseverare in esse suo*) as merely the lowest stratum in a much more complex and far more debatable concept of the human end or good of man.[8]

Hart's attenuation, however, has less to do with the content of natural law than with its framework. He does wish to exclude metaphysics more than, I think, is warranted, but except for this, he is very much in line with a formulation of much of the second table of the Decalogue although he does not say exactly the same thing. Hart's suggestions for a minimum content of natural law are:

> 1) Because, and as long as men are vulnerable, law and morality will have to "restrict the use of violence in killing or inflicting bodily harm."
> 2) Because men are approximately equal, there must be "a system of mutual forbearance and compromise" which is the base of both legal and moral obligation.
> 3) Because men are neither devils nor angels, there must be a measure of human altruism.
> 4) Because the earth provides limited resources, that fact makes "indispensable some minimal form of the institution of property (though not necessarily individual property) and the distinctive kind of rule which requires it."
> 5) Because of the darker side of man's nature 'sanctions' are . . . required not as the normal motive for obedience but as a guarantee that those who would voluntarily obey shall not be sacrificed to those who would not . . . Given this standing danger, what reason demands is voluntary co-operation in a coercive system.[9]

It should be noticed immediately that Hart is speaking not of mere physical survival, but of survival in community. Indeed, it would make no sense to speak of *mores* at all unless one were speaking of a community.

To this extent, Hart's procedure and his conclusions are familiar ones but there are notable omissions from Hart's list, perhaps implicit in numbers two and three. In addition to restriction of death-dealing (number one on Hart's list) and some institution of property (number four), Thomas, for one, would want to include some organization of sexual life which would provide for the education of children and the care of the elderly (the fourth, sixth and ninth commandments). Truth telling is effectively covered in Hart's discussion of his fourth category, not clear in the paraphrase given above. These omissions seem peculiar and may indicate the limitations of what Hart means by survival—so that survival is a matter of individuals and procreation is either a physical need like avoidance of pain or a luxury over and above one's individual survival. To the extent that he is talking of societies, and of moral language, the omissions seem inexplicable.

These omissions should not obscure for us the formal structure of Hart's argument. He proceeds with two sets of assertions. The first assertion is that of a universal characteristic of humanity, the desire for survival. The second is the set of classes of things which inevitably follow if humans are to survive in this world. Hart, however, does not want to see this desire for survival as in any way necessary for man, that is, he does not want to make the desire for survival into a metaphysical category. Rather, he sees it as a merely "contingent" fact about humanity.

It is not clear that Hart can avoid such metaphysics, however. He seems to mean that whereas man is under no compulsion to desire survival, that desire is strong enough so that it is the central premise of all human mores:

> We may hold it to be a mere contingent fact, which could be otherwise, that in general men do desire to live, and that we may mean nothing more by calling survival a human good or end than that men do desire it.[10]

Such a formulation would be quite foreign to Thomas Aquinas, who believed that things which inevitably happen, happen by necessity, and it seems that his position can be at least partially defended in this case. Hart wishes to say that the desire for survival is not inevitable and thus not necessary but it is clear that where the desire for survival is not a part of man, we can no longer speak of man as we know him. It must certainly mean something of man as we know him that he inevitably chooses to place high value on survival.[11]

That Hart's listing of the contents of natural law should closely resemble the categories of actions mentioned in the Decalogue—the ten commandments—is not surprising. The second table of the Decalogue—or more properly the classes which these embody—seem to correspond to the constants in human cultures that anthropologists have isolated. David Little, summarizing Kluckholm, notes the following "ethical universals":

> a) prohibitions against murder (wanton killing within the in-group), as distinguished from other forms of justifiable homicide; b) prohibitions against stealing within the in-group; c) prohibitions against incest and other regulations on sexual behavior; d) prohibition under defined circumstances against lying; e) regulations and stipulations regarding restitution and reciprocity of property; f) stipulations of mutual obligations between parent and children.[12]

As Little notes, the resemblances between this list and the second table of the Decalogue are striking.

On the other hand, Hart's listing includes a greater awareness of the societal nature of concepts of duty and the like than does Thomas'. In his second category Hart speaks of the obviousness of "a system of mutual forbearance and compromise which is the basis of both legal and moral obligation." Again, in his fifth category, he notes:

> neither understanding of long-term interest, nor the strength of goodness of will, upon which the efficacy of these different motives toward obedience (to moral and legal rules) depends, are shared by all men alike. All are tempted at times to prefer their own immediate interests and in the absence of a special organization for their detection and punishment, many would succumb to the temptation . . . Given this standing danger, what reason demands is *voluntary* co-operation in a *coercive* system.[13]

One of the troubles with Hart's formulations is, in fact, this subordination of "moral and legal rules" to the matter of survival. Most natural law theories place the inclination to morality at the springs of natural law, from which all else follows. By placing survival alone in that key position, and making a sense of morality a consequence of survival, Hart seems to be doing more than merely putting the cart before the horse. In spite of his avowal of the contingency of survival, he is making a serious metaphysical assumption. Either he is committing the naturalistic fallacy in a latter-day Hobbesian way, or he is using the word *survival* in such a large, vague way as to make it no improvement on the metaphysics he wishes to eschew.

Thomas Aquinas

It is in this emphasis upon survival alone as the source of natural law that Hart is least like Thomas Aquinas. In other respects the differences between them are less considerable. A careful reading of the "Treatise on Law," free of the interpolation of ideas from the earlier work of Thomas in the *Commentum* shows a surprising degree of agreement with Hart. Certainly they proceed in formally the same fashion. Thomas posits 'natural inclinations' of human beings and, of course, posits more than only survival, and considers them more than 'mere contingent' facts. From these he proceeds to the Decalogue. He is even willing, unlike Hart, to move even closer into the area of specificity. He seems to have in mind a breakdown of natural law such as the following: 1) The first principle of the practical reason, that is, good is to be done and evil is to be avoided, which follows from the recognition of what 'good' means; 2) Precepts of natural law, which follow from recognition of certain specific goods. These specific goods are the objects of 'natural inclinations'. 3) Secondary precepts, which are more specific than the precepts and which are compared to conclusions which follow from first principles.[14] In the previous chapter we looked at the first of these, the "principle" according to which persons seek to do good and avoid evil. For the moment let us look at the second, the natural inclinations of human beings and the precepts to which they lead. The commandments of the Decalogue are involved here, though in a rather special way, and here we see the resemblances and differences with Hart most clearly. The temptation with the first principles of action is to expect them to be unquestionably true the way the first principles of speculation are. For Thomas, however, they are not statements at all, but judgments of good. They are not unquestionable truths but unquestionable goods. The analogy he sees between the principles of the speculative reason and those of the practical reason lies in the fact that both must be presupposed if any other judgments are to be made. They are unquestionable in the sense that, although they cannot be proved, they are necessary and must be taken for granted.

To our ears both the word precepts and the notion of natural inclinations, a term we shall now consider, may sound strange. "Precepts" in fact seems to presuppose a very rationalistic way of approaching the question and has an obvious relationship to the concept of God that Thomas is accepting. In fact, Thomas does not state the precepts as such; he approaches them in a less rationalistic way by calling them natural inclinations. Thomas' theory of natural inclinations is an attempt to explain the origins of such judgments of goodness. But although they function as explanations inasmuch as they fit Thomas' theory into the general framework of his doctrine of appetite, they are superfluous inasmuch as they add nothing to the unquestionability of the precepts. Theoretical explanations of why the first principles are true are attempts to get behind one's own starting point and are in the same class as speculation about why being should be such that there is no affirming and denying the same simultaneously. Whereas for Hart, all of natural morality follows from the desire for survival, for Thomas this desire is one of several that humans naturally have. He lists these desires in an organic hierarchy:

> Because in man there is first of all an inclination to good in accordance with the nature which he has in common with all substances: inasmuch as every substance seeks the preservation of its own being, according to its nature: and by reason of this whatever is a means of preserving human life and of warding off its obstacles, belong to the natural law.
>
> Secondly there is in man an inclination to things that pertain to him more specially, according to that nature which he has in common with other animals: and in virtue of this inclination those things are said to belong to the natural law which nature teaches all animals, such as sexual intercourse, education of offspring and so forth.
>
> Thirdly there is in man an inclination to good, according to the nature of his reason, which nature is proper to him: thus man has a natural inclination toward those things which lead him to the truth about God and to those things which enable him to live in society: and in this respect, whatever pertains to this inclination belongs to the natural law; for instance to shun ignorance, to avoid offending those among whom one has to live, and other such things regarding the above inclinations.[15]

The wording of this passage is significant in that Thomas speaks first of the recognition of a good and then of the matter which "belongs to natural law" (*pertinent ad legem naturalem . . . de lege naturali . . . ad legem naturalem pertinent*). The process he seems to have in mind is the recognition 'X is good' which is the same as 'X ought to be done' as a result of the first principle.

The goods which Thomas recognizes are rather difficult to paraphrase, partly because of the unclarity of Thomas' second category. It is not clear whether the need for food is seen as a necessity of survival or one of the things which nature "teaches all animals." It seems probable, given the history of the phrase, its euphemistic tone, and the examples with which Thomas follows it that he would include under the second category only matters of sexuality and of bringing up the young. At any rate into the first two categories of good would fall three general classes of things:

1) Survival
2) Health and physical well-being
3) The continuation of the species

Thomas seems to have intended to have included only the last of these three in his own second category, but the three headings are, anyway, an accurate recapitulation of his thought. The second category might be put better in the negative as 'avoidance of pain' and should be taken in that sense, but as Thomas uses the affirmative I will retain his usage.

Thomas' third category relates to the good of human beings, considered as persons. This is very problematic and all of the difficulties of recognizing the happiness of man, to which we shall return in the next chapter, come into this category.

The two goods to which we are naturally inclined as specific to human beings are then:

4) To know the truth about God
5) To live in society

In the question following this one, Thomas names another such good, to act according to reason, but this is really a corollary of the first principle rather than a separate inclination of human beings.

Shunning ignorance, however, he thinks is a part of our natural inclination to know the truth about God.

These are the goods which Thomas enumerates as being recognized by all men and from them we know the precepts of the natural law. Given the vagueness of the description of these goods it is not surprising that Thomas speaks of these precepts as being "general principles" or "most general precepts" (*communia principia . . . praecepta communissima*).[16]

According to Thomas, then, there are precepts of natural law which are no more than recognition that the above goods are to be done and their contraries avoided, but there are also slight specifications of these which, while not precepts of natural law, are nevertheless clear to all. In discussing the ten commandments he notes that the Decalogue is a kind of middle ground between the precepts of natural law and the more particular precepts which he sometimes calls "secondary." It is important to note that the recognition of these goods Thomas considers to be universal, true of all persons, or rather, all societies. His assertion here is thus a metaphysical one about man's experience of himself in the world. We everywhere recognize these basic goods because we everywhere experience the world in the same way.

First of all, it may come as some surprise to note that Thomas does not include the Decalogue among the precepts of natural law. They are a special kind of secondary precept. The most general precepts are more self-evident, since they are nothing but the recognition of our natural inclinations. The commandments of the Decalogue are obvious "with but slight reflection." The recognition of the worth of other persons and of society, in other words, is more general and more obvious than the specifications of what that recognition means which we identify as the second table of the Decalogue. Moreover, Thomas can include in this special category those commandments of the Decalogue that pertain directly to God, for unlike Hart he predicates a natural human inclination toward Him.[17] To use a more symbolic language than that of precepts, the essential human virtues—for Thomas, prudence, justice, fortitude, and temperance, but also faith, hope, and charity—are a matter of natural inclination and are thus of a higher degree of universality than even the Decalogue itself. What he seems to have in mind is that the most general principles can be known by all, and with them can be known certain other statements which we understand as soon as we understand the terms, but that these terms are themselves in need of great specification. Thus, if we understand terms such as disrespect, murder, stealing, and the like, we can see that they are contrary to reason. This is so because the terms are the names of evil actions. We thus can come to know not to murder, because murder is unjust killing, but we need to be instructed as to what counts as murder. We have thus statements we automatically recognize as true because they are tautologous, but we need to have the tautologies eliminated by the wise.[18]

The first class of secondary precepts of which Thomas speaks, then, are those which include the precepts of the Decalogue. These are *per se nota* after slight consideration. But they are tautologous. Thomas' own explication of the fifth commandment of the Decalogue is:

> The slaying of someone is forbidden in the decalogue insofar as it bears the character of something undue: for in this sense the precept contains the very essence of justice . . . Accordingly, therefore, the precepts of the decalogue, as to the essence of justice which they contain, are unchangeable; but as to any determination by application to individual actions—for instance that this or that be murder, theft, or adultery or not—in this point they admit of change; sometimes by Divine authority alone, namely in such matters as are exclusively of Divine institution, as marriage and the like; sometimes also by human authority, namely in such matters as are subject to human jurisdiction: for in this respect men stand in the place of God: and yet not in all respects.[19]

Drawing back from the text for a moment we note that for Thomas the self-evident (*per se nota*) precepts of natural law are so very general that they do not include even such specifications as 'murder is evil'. This latter type of statement is what the Decalogue contains, but the Decalogue is already out of the classification of *per se nota* precepts of natural law.

It should not need too much stressing that, if Thomas himself saw that the Decalogue is a series of tautological statements, he must also have seen that they are of little use in leading to specific rules of conduct. Thomas seems clearly to mean that:

'murder is evil'

is to be read as saying that:

'unjust killing (of a human) is evil'

but that is simply to say that X = X since the moral term 'unjust' (or murder) and the moral term 'evil' entail one another and appear on both sides of the copulative. It is important to note that Thomas begins in the passage quoted above with the non-moral term 'kill', but quickly switches to murder—as well as to 'theft' and 'adultery'—in order to make this point.

In summary of what we have been so far regarding Thomas' doctrine of natural law we should note the following points, returning first to the first principle:

1) The first principle of the practical reason is distinct from the precepts of the natural law inasmuch as it is entirely a matter of coming to know what it is to make a practical judgment. (In it, however, Thomas places his explanation of the reason why men are concerned with morals. Concern with morals is part of the seeking after happiness which is characteristic of man. This side of this theory is important, but for the time being we are concerned more with the consequences of man's coming to recognize a good.)
2) Certain things are always recognized as good by men. Thomas says not only that they always are so recognized, but that the explanation of why they are so recognized is part of the nature of man.
3) The goods Thomas identifies as characteristic of man as a person are the seeking after truth and living in community, to which he adds acting according to reason. Seeking after happiness, already included in the first principle should undoubtedly be otherwise counted here.
4) The precepts of the natural law are judgments which we automatically make as a result of recognizing goods and the first principle. Thus if they were stated as precepts they would read something like the following:
   a. Whatever is necessary to survival should be sought after and done.

b. Pain should be avoided.
c. Children ought to be conceived, borne, and educated.
d. Truth should be sought after; Thomas states this negatively as ignorance should be shunned. He also implies theologically that seeking after God is natural to man.
e. Whatever is necessary for life in community should be done. Thomas states this negatively as "Do evil to no man."
f. Acting contrary to reason should be avoided.

5) Among the secondary precepts there are certain "proximate conclusions" of the precepts which Thomas believes to be only slightly less immediately obvious than the precepts. These are the commandments of the Decalogue, here meaning the second table. They are always tautologies which involve substitutions of good or evil as both subject and predicate. In this tautologous sense Thomas considers them as knowable by all.

If Thomas had said no more than what we have already discussed, natural law would be a relatively uncontroversial doctrine. It would be equivalent to saying that there are certain constants in all moral reasoning but that these are extremely general. Even the slightly less general precepts, which are not so self-evident as these most general (*communissimus*) precepts, are also very vague, although they do identify the areas in which specification is needed.

Up to this point, as I have said, Thomas' doctrine seems to be no more than a description of the constants in human moral systems. If natural law is to have a practical value we must be able to move from these generalities to rules of conduct. Yet here Thomas is very unclear. He says that we can arrive at rules of conduct in either of two ways:

> Something may be derived from the natural law in two ways: first, as a conclusion from premises, secondly, by way of determination of certain generalities . . . Some things therefore are derived from the general principles of the natural law by way of conclusions; e.g., that one must not kill may be derived as a conclusion from the principle that one should do harm to no man: while some are arrived therefrom by way of determination; e.g., the law of nature has it that the evildoer should

> be punished, but that he be punished in this or that way, is a determination of the law of nature.[20]

Since Thomas says a few questions later, in a passage I have already quoted, that the counsels of the wise are needed to determine whether this or that killing be murder, we seem to arrive at the same point by either method. The way of proceeding to conclusions gives the appearance of being based on a 'practical syllogism'. Such a syllogism begins with the statement "do evil to no man" which he says leads to the conclusion "do no murder." Presumably the middle step would be 'murder is evil' and so a syllogism would be formed. In human law, Thomas maintains that secondary precepts derived in this latter manner "have some force from natural law" while those derived in the former, by determination, do not.[21] This seems to mean that statements such as those of the Decalogue are binding in natural law, whereas determinations of these are matters of human law. This usage seems to contradict the many passages where Thomas speaks of anything which reason commands as being of natural law and indicates the ambiguities which follow from his ambiguous position on the number of the precepts. Closer examination of the passage indicates that what Thomas means is that those things which are *necessarily true* are of natural law. The other class of things is comprised of cases where reason directs that *something* be done, but where specification is, by comparison, arbitrary. This latter case is not of natural law.

This twofold method of arriving at secondary precepts does not exhaust all that Thomas says about such principles. He also says:

1) they are not the same for all, nor known by all[22]
2) they may be added to[23]
3) they can be blotted out in the human heart[24]
4) sometimes not knowing secondary precepts is a matter of guilt, sometimes only of error.[25]

Thomas is consistent in ascribing variability to the secondary precepts and in identifying them with the judgments of the wise, or human law[26] although he does not draw out the implications as consistently as he might have.

Thomas does not identify secondary precepts of the natural law with human law because he uses the latter term in a non-analogical sense to mean laws promulgated by human political authority. Had he used the term to refer to laws framed by men, or rules known by the human mind, however, human law would coincide with secondary precepts of the natural law. The latter include, for Thomas, all that reason tells us about the living of our lives. The contrast between human law and natural law in Thomas' usage is that the one is the result of human political processes and the latter is the result of human reason. Thomas thus allows for the possibility of conflict between human law and man's moral judgment. When there is a conflict between the two, the latter is always the one to be followed, for man should always act according to reason. Thomas' argument here is interesting inasmuch as Thomas identifies acting according to reason as acting according to the natural law:

> As Augustine says (*De Lib. Arb.* 1.5) that which is not just seems to be no law at all: wherefore the force of a law depends on the extent of its justice. Now in human affairs a thing is said to be just from being right, according to the rule of reason. But the first rule of reason is the natural law, as is clear from what has been stated above. Consequently every human law has just so much of the nature of law as it is derived from the law of nature. But if in any point it deflects from the law of nature, it is no longer a law but a perversion of law.[27]

As we have seen, Thomas' notion of the universal precepts of natural law seem to be very vague and potentially flexible. He himself does not see any problem in moving from these general notions to specific content, but for us the gap between the unchangeable precepts and the secondary precepts derived from them is glaringly wide. Into that gap Thomas puts the reflections of the wise, the promulgation of just rulers, divine positive law, and, above all, human reason. It is because the latter inclines us to act according to virtue that Thomas is able to build upon natural law, but he does so not in the direction of a definition of acts, but in the direction of the disposition of the moral subject.[28]

The chief exception Thomas makes to this transition to speaking of virtue is with regard to temperance and the nature of sexuality. What he does here is switch from speaking of human nature, our *humanum,* to human nature considered as our body. Thus a potential conflict between what human reason inclines toward and the nature of the human body is prepared for. The results of this conflict are too well known to need reiterating. There is a sense in which the human body establishes the parameters of what seems reasonable for a human being to attempt to do, but the knowledge of these parameters cannot logically stand outside of human reason. Everywhere else Thomas sensibly opts for a natural law that inclines human beings to act according to reason; only with regard to sex does he fall into a natural law of acts rather than of virtues. It is a mistake which can be explained by reference to the tradition, but it cannot be justified. He makes the transition in the following passage:

> By human nature we may mean either that which is proper to man—and in this sense all sins, as being against reason, are also against nature, as Damascene says: or we may mean that nature which is common to man and other animals; and in this sense, certain special sins are said to be against nature; thus contrary to sexual intercourse, which is natural to all animals, is unisexual lust, which has received the special name of the unnatural crime.[29]

But aside from this exception, Thomas is quite willing to use the vague "advice of the wise" to explain how the precepts are to be made specific. The category *per se nota* to the wise is a mysterious one.

Per Se Nota Sapientibus

To proceed closer toward the area of content is a risky task. A considerable amount of literature—philosophical, theological and even sociological and anthropological—could be cited in defense of the general outlines of the theory so far described. But attempts to go further than this have been, so far as I know, quite rare and always tied to a particular conclusion the author wishes to advance. Little or no attention has been paid to the general form of the theory as Thomas advanced it.

This is quite understandable, for Thomas is quite unclear about the derivation of secondary precepts of natural law and, in fact, himself made no attempt to set out an ethics based on it in his own *Summa*. The "Special Ethics" section of the *S.T.* (II-II) is organized around the three theological and four cardinal virtues, not around the precepts of natural law.

But to proceed further, although it may be temerarious, might be to uncover some truth about what is usually called natural law and even to bring a step closer the presently disparate worlds of linguistic philosophers, utilitarians, and perhaps, theologians.

What I would like to suggest is not new. It is an analysis of Thomas' *per se nota* judgments already suggested by Victor Preller in his study of Thomas' natural theology, and Preller himself relies heavily on the work of Wilfred Sellars.[30]

In talking about the ways in which we arrive at proximate rules of conduct from natural law Thomas says:

> For there are certain things which the natural reason of every man, of its own accord and at once, judges to be done or not to be done: e.g., honor they father and thy mother, and thou shalt not kill, thou shalt not steal: and these belong to the law of nature absolutely. And there are certain things which, after a more careful consideration, wise men deem obligatory. Such belong to the law of nature, yet so that they need to be inculcated. The wiser teaching the less wise.[31]

A way out of this cul-de-sac may be suggested by an examination of the *per se nota* judgment. Some judgments that Thomas designates as such would be today called analytic judgments; Thomas uses the example, "Man is a rational being."[32] Such a statement is for Thomas an explicit definition. Other such statements, particularly those Thomas calls *per se nota* to the wise, would today be called synthetic *a priori* judgments. Thus the judgment that an angel is not conscriptively in a place is *per se nota* to those who know that an angel is not a body. The present status of the analytic/synthetic distinction seems to be such that to say that a *per se nota* truth is a synthetic *a priori* is to replace an enigma with a conundrum, but the situation could be clarified.

The question of the synthetic *a priori* is whether a statement can be necessarily true and yet not be merely logically true. That is, can a statement be necessarily true and true *of experience?* Wilfred Sellars' answer to the problem will not appeal to most Thomists or to most empiricists, but to those who accept the post-Kantian premise that intelligibility is dictated by the conceptual and syntactical structures of our minds it makes inevitable sense. The chief difficulty such a position has for Thomists—aside from those explicitly related to epistemology or to philosophy of mind—is in the area of the theoretical reformulability of human language, a problem we have already discussed.

The position that Sellars maintains is surprisingly similar to that expressed by Thomas himself in his *Commentary on the Posterior Analytics of Aristotle.* There Thomas, following Aristotle, observes that any science (i.e., roughly, any organized body of knowledge) cannot be formulated unless it is built on the base of certain unquestionable truths. That is, contingent judgments can only be made if there is a relation, implicit or explicit, to necessary ones. In Thomas' somewhat crude example the science of medicine might include the truth that a certain drug cured fever. This statement would itself be the result of repeated observations that the drug cured fever which would then be taken by the mind as the unconditionally assertable truth, 'this drug cures fever'. He says:

> Reason does not terminate in the experience of particulars, but from many particulars of experience, it grasps one common thing, which is confirmed by the mind and considers it without reference to the particulars upon which it was founded; and this common thing it takes as the principle of the art and the science. . . .[33]

Thomas' (and Aristotle's) point, put briefly, is that in order for us to be able to refer to experience intelligibly there must be some statement that we make or imply about experience that we take for granted. Sellars' position is akin to that of Thomas, but his framework is that of the language we use to refer to reality. He would say, for example, that the reason we can move from 'This is an apple' to 'This is edible' is because the conceptual status of 'apple' in our language is such that 'all apples are edible' is an unconditionally assertable proposition in our language. (I am speaking hypothetically, not as a pharmacist.) He says:

> . . . where 'X is B' can be validly inferred from 'X is A,' the proposition 'all A is B' is unconditionally assertable on the basis of the rules of the language. Our thesis, then, implies that every primitive descriptive predicate occurs in one or more logically synthetic propositions which are unconditionally assertable–in short, true *ex vi terminorum.*[34]

Sellars' use of the Latin tag *ex vi terminorum* is felicitous for our purposes, for *per se nota* and *ex vi terminorum nota* are similar enough in meaning to indicate how closely the two concepts are related. The frame of reference in which he and Thomas operate is sufficiently close that he himself defends in one essay "The profound truth contained in the Thomistic thesis that the senses in their way and the intellect in its way are informed by the natures of external objects and events," although he does not *entirely* agree with this position.[35]

The point that Sellars is making is not likely to endear him either to traditional Kantians or to traditional Thomists, however. For though he thus arrives at a notion that is very similar to that of a truth *per se nota sapientibus* or a synthetic *a priori,* his truth *ex vi terminorum* is different in one important respect. His unconditionally assertable truth is unconditionally assertable in *a given language.* It is always theoretically possible that a set of conditions could arise in which the unconditionally assertable truth no longer was found useful and therefore was discarded. Just as, in Thomas' example, a significant number of cases in which the given drug did not cure fever would lead one to stop using 'this drug cures fever' as an unconditionally true statement, so it is theoretically possible that any *ex vi terminorum* truth could be similarly discarded.

It is difficult to imagine some of these statements disappearing—every event must have a cause, for example. But a quick glance at some of the findings of anthropologists cautions anyone against being too certain of his judgments.

The point towards which I have been driving has finally come into sight. The mystifiying distinction between the extremely general precepts of natural law and these secondary precepts which are the result of the cogitations of the wise can now, I think, be understood. The former are clearly intended by Thomas to be true in all societies and to be knowable by all. The latter, however,

Thomas consistently taught could be different for different men (he uses the example of a different *culture*), may be added to, can be blotted out in the human heart and could be unknown to the agent without his guilt.[36] Given his insistance that they are dependent on the wisdom of man and these admissions of variability, it is an extrapolation from Thomas, but one certainly justified by the text, to see these specifications as culturally or historically variable. While the more general precepts are universal, the secondary precepts are *per se nota* only within their given frame of reference.

Of course, Sellars' point is a widely acknowledged one today but one which is considerably clearer when applied to judgments of truth than to judgments of goodness. What I am suggesting is that the latter are embedded in the presuppositons of a language in a way analogous to the former. It is to be hoped that someday we will have a clearer understanding of the way social arrangements set the parameters of what is considered moral. At present sociologists have only begun to explore this kind of social causality. But living in the times we do, we all have a sense of the ways in which questions of life or death vary with the state of medical knowledge and technology, the way contraceptive technology has altered our sexual customs or the way military developments such as atomic or chemical-biological warfare have thrown askew the traditional doctrine of war.

Between the vague generalities that Thomas called natural law and the specific customs and morals of a given community there stretches a chain of assumptions, conclusions and decisions which, if we knew it, would explain to us why there is so much variety to human understanding of the good and the right. What appears reasonable under conditions X is likely to be different than what appears reasonable under conditions Y.

Such a formulation suggests more possibility of change than is usually associated with Thomas. I do not deny that for him the practices of his own culture and his own contributions as a wise man were normative or that, for example, the polygamy of the patriarchs was an embarrassment to him. Two different kinds of argument can nevertheless be made to justify this interpretation.

The first is that Thomas himself in his more strictly theological moments talked of the difference between truth as it exists in the mind of man and truth as it exists in God and postulated the merely analogous nature of human truth. His clearest exposition of this theme is in *de Veritate,* although it can be found in discussions of the knowledge of the angels, the knowledge of Christ and man's knowledge of himself in the *Summa Theologiae.* As we have seen, a close examination of the virtues of *synderesis* and *intellectus principiorum* would indicate their function as bridging this gap in a minimal way in Thomas' theological scheme. A discussion of analogy in Thomas seems unnecesssary at this point since, *whatever the degree of analogy* he intended in the analogy of truth, it is clear that any admission of the analogous status of our knowledge is an admission of at least some theoretical reformulability.

Within the body of Thomas' work also the finely drawn distinction between precepts of natural law and secondary precepts is more clearly apparent than in that of any of his commentators. It is significant, I think, that Thomas himself does not use the common distinction between primary and secondary precepts in his late work; in the *Summa* the distinction is between precepts of natural law and more particular precepts, which he occasionally refers to as secondary. The exploratory power of the suggestion that I have made is clearer in Thomas than in the natural law of the tradition.

Secondly, the history of Christian ethics is such that some such provision for change as I have suggested is needed to explain for the changes particular positions have taken over the years. Quite independently of whether my suggestion can be legitimately applied to Thomas, it seems to me to be a necessity for anyone who would explain Christianity's changing attitudes toward, let us say, usury, the justifications of intercourse, the relations of citizens to empire, feudal lord, king, or democratic government. One need only remember the gingerliness of the tradition's handling of patriarchal polygamy or the conciliar condemnation of lending money for interest to see my point here.

I am maintaining that the general form of Thomas' theory of natural law is correct, but that a careful reading of his text shows a considerable logical jump between a set of vague but important generalities and any specific ethical norms. These latter, I suggest, can be called natural law not in the sense that they are natural to all persons everywhere, but in the extended sense of that term which Thomas consistently identifies with human reason. To one who stood within the thirteenth century a certain set of *per se nota* judgments seemed to be so certain as to be unquestionable, but they are in theory quite questionable, even replaceable. The criterion of such judgments is reason, and this is, indeed, the main theological point Thomas establishes in his discussion of natural law. Endless quotations could be used to illustrate this conclusion which Thomas repeated over and over:

> Since human morals depend on their relation to reason, which is the proper principle of human acts, those morals are called good which accord with reason, and those are called bad which are discordant from reason.[37]

What Makes Sense

We are not living in a time of stable moral conventions. When Thomas spoke of specifications of moral codes being the province of the wise, he may have had in mind figures like Augustine whose judgments had been normative in establishing the morality of the medieval world. Thomas himself has, of course, assumed that role for many in history subsequent to him. Closer to our own time we may think of Jefferson or Mill as figures influential in establishing some of the mores of our own society. But we are likely to think less in terms of towering figures than in terms of arrival at a democratic consensus, at least within limited communities, as the basis of moral codes which will meet the needs of our own times with its unprecedented technology and the problems it brings. Such a consensus has always been at least implicit in the idea that morality is natural to human beings, and therefore we are, in any case, forced into the shadowy area of individual decision-making.

One of the key concepts unexplained so far in our deliberations has been the one which explains how human beings come to recognize what they eventually are willing to call good action or even 'the good'. Up until a century or so ago it was widely thought that such a process of recognition could be described as reasonable or rational.[38] But since then the 'rational basis of morality' has been more and more understood to mean the claim that morality could be based simply on descriptive language, and continuous attacks have been made upon such a basis. Into the vacuum thus created have flown theories of the emotional basis of morality, which in the temper of the times came to mean its arbitrariness, its basis in mere subjective whim. It might almost be said that the basis of morals was for a while understood as being either the heteronomous decisions of an outside community or an autonomy based in nothing but mere abitrariness. Nietzsche, for example, seems to have wanted to understand morality thus. I have been using the descriptive category 'what makes sense' and it is time that we spent some time examining this concept. In terms of the understanding of human morality I have been trying to present, it is not enough to speak of what makes sense as being rational in the conventional sense of that term. There is something right about the term *rational,* but we must beware of overextending its use in matters that concern the experienced life of human beings (experience is, of course, a broader category than reason). In dealing with human beings and with human behavior, we must recognize that decisions how to live a unique life cannot be explained simply in terms of the 'given' historical world. Although those of us who write books of this kind and those of us who read them are perhaps dedicated to maximizing the influence of reason in ourselves and to using the term *reason* to mean that which can be objectively proven, we must admit that reason in this sense is a culture-bound category, that which counts as reasonable in our time and place may not have seemed thus a century ago or would not seem reasonable somewhere else and may not seem so tomorrow even here. In spite of our appeals to reasonableness, we are nevertheless stuck in the peculiar intellectual problem of the late twentieth century, that of cultural relativism.[39]

If there is a way out of this well-known dilemma, it must include both an objective and a subjective element. On the one hand, human beings seem to need to believe that they are in touch with the real objective world. In fact, the desire to be good is a real objective fact about human beings, and that desire for goodness can always be expressed at least vaguely—as an understanding of justice, for example. On the other hand, our understanding of the world must make sense in terms of our own subjective experience. Perhaps the greatest theorist of this ambiguity has been the psychologist William James with his careful analysis of ideas about the world and the ways in which such ideas must survive continuous testing against reality as experienced by individuals and groups in a wide variety of modes.[40] If James and other American pragmatists are not well-known today, it may be a sign that their understanding of the historical situation of human beings runs even more against our prejudices than they already suspected.

Another way of raising the same issue is a bit closer to us in time. Many attempts have been made to interpret the social context of human knowledge, and perhaps in the long run Marx's theses on Feuerbach remains the classic text in this respect. But one of the most widely known American theorists of the sociology of knowledge is Peter L. Berger, who with Thomas Luckmann wrote the widely known exposition of this theme, *The Social Construction of Reality.*[41] One of the dynamics of knowledge Berger and Luckmann consider most important is the dynamic between the ways in which human beings are shaped by their environment and yet are able to creatively change that environment. In order to explain this creative interplay the authors found necessary an explanation of human beings which allowed a margin of individuality over and above the particularities of the personality which could be attributed to the community. This margin of individuality provides also a certain degree of freedom with respect to the group and an area of anxiety when the individual becomes conscious of his or her lack of integration into the meaning-giving community. In terms of our analysis this serves simply to remind us that what is reasonable seems to be a function of whatever community one seems to belong to and that in spite of long-standing human attempts to arrive at a truth which is not susceptible to this kind of criticism, all of the social sciences seem still to fall under this criticism.

For the purpose of this study, such a relativism is not disquieting. We must over and over again assert that human beings act according to what makes sense to them in the particular circumstances of their particular lives—or at least they try to. But if reasonable means 'in accordance with the conventions of a particular social group' are we then saying that people act *only* in accordance with the conventions of the social groups in which they find themselves? Clearly this is frequently the case, but it is also clear that such a relativism makes nonsense of the usual claims that natural law makes about human reasoning. One way out of the dilemma and the way which has been chosen most insistently in our recent Western traditions has been the attempt to fight our way through conventional thinking to arrive at that which can be rationally shown to be really true. This insistence that human reason is able to adequately describe the ultimate nature of things has been one of the glories of Western civilization and has, especially, been the source of the scientific method, which is certainly one of humanity's greatest accomplishments. The importance of the scientific method and the drive for human acquisition of ultimate truth which it embodies can hardly be overestimated and ought not to be minimized even in the face of its excesses. The empirical testing of hypotheses about reality, which is the heart of scientific method, is a refinement of human understanding which is invaluable. With such testing against reality we may even be able to learn from the very excesses which the scientific method itself has brought on, especially the shrinking of the human spirit.

The other extreme, opposed to the attempt to come to an intellectual knowledge of ultimate reality, has been to deny the usefulness of reason and to emphasize the basic correctness of the orientation of the human heart. Proponents of such a view, when they are not given to excessive individualism, will point out that the accomplishments of human reason are useless unless they are able to affect the lives of ordinary persons in an ordinary way. Moreover, they rightly assert that many of the accomplishments of humans that we most value (including the concept of *value*) cannot be explained solely in terms of human reason. The Parthenon and Chartres Cathedral, they say, were less a product of calculating reason than of the ability of humans to grasp in a more than logical way some principle of order in the universe.

Both positions seem to have a certain amount of truth as well as a certain danger. We ought not to be forced to be in a situation where we must choose between the scientific method and Chartres Cathedral as the true expression of the human spirit. Human reason alone seems to be dominant right now and its pursuit of efficiency seems more and more to emphasize those qualities of human beings which proclaim our capacity to be manipulated and palliated. Left to its own devices the human heart seems as likely to produce the stupor of a spectator or the rage of a mob as the glories of Chartres Cathedral.

All of this should be borne in mind as we try to analyze what it means to talk about the things that make sense regarding human action. In a climate which emphasizes the deductively rational, an attempt to explain the human moral response must emphasize the affective and the intuitive, but to do so is not to surrender the inevitable and necessary reflection upon experience which is just as surely one of the characteristics of human beings.[42]

To be a human being is to try to make sense of a large amount of extraordinarily various information about the world and about ourselves. From our senses, our emotions, our intelligence and our intuition we receive frequently contradictory data. As sensory beings desiring pleasure and survival and hating pain, as emotional beings needing other persons and groups of persons, and as intelligent beings seeking to become worthwhile individuals, we are pulled in all sorts of directions and sometimes, it seems, in all directions at once. To say of a pattern of behavior that it makes sense to a person is to say that it seems to satisfy enough of these various inclinations to appear to be the right thing to do. Such a judgment of rightness is partly an intellectual decision and partly a not easily analyzed sense of congruence between one's conduct and one's understanding of the world, and both of these perceptions must be measured against one another. Our intelligence must measure our sense of congruence and our non-intellectual knowledge of the world must judge our reasoning about it.

Such an understanding of human activity would be a great deal easier to explain if human beings were not typically in such a flux about exactly what makes sense to them. It was a commonplace of the medieval world that every individual human being was a microcosm, containing in herself all of the significant elements of the physical world. It may help in understanding the theory of natural law to adapt this metaphor. In this adaptation we would say that each individual is a microcommunity and that each of us contains all of the senses of the world which any of us can contain. Like a parliament coming to a consensus, we determine what seems to us the best behavior in the world. And perhaps if we take the metaphor seriously, we can understand how other parliaments—other persons—can arrive at different consensuses about human behavior.

Acting reasonably, doing what makes sense, is always a matter of balancing various kinds of claims that are made on our attention. For purposes of discussion we might talk of a spectrum of behaviors which we find reasonable or acceptable and we might note that the spectrum moves from a range of actions that we would call self-centered or even selfish, to a range that is centered on others, that is altruistic and communitarian. Both in the individual and in the society there seems to be a necessity to accept the importance of both of these two polar concerns and to arrive at a manner of behaving that is an acceptable compromise between them. In occasional individual moments we may find ourselves acting considerably more self-centeredly or altruistically than we usually do and both as individuals and as members of society we are aware of the potential instability of our moral compromises.

One of the places where the Christian moralist will object to this sketch of ordinary morality is precisely here. One of the forces which motivates people to act more altruistically is that they are encouraged to do so by one another and specifically in the name of a higher morality. I am not denying this difference between a more altruistic Christian morality and the ordinary morality of most people most of the time. Is it not the case, however, that persons can only respond to the appeals of Christian morality if they have the capacity to understand that appeal?[43] In other words, even in acting more altruistically than usual their behavior still makes sense to them. To insist that morality is based in reality is not to deny the complexities of moral decisions either for individuals or for whole groups. It is rather to insist that morality arises out of the human need to make sense of their lives and this need must be tempered against the real world and the real subjectivity of the agent. Given this tempering, only a range of behavior makes sense and very frequently people will need to be encouraged to act in a way more directed towards other persons than towards themselves. The relationship between Christian morality and natural morality is a dynamic one but both kinds of behavior are rooted in the ordinary experience of ordinary persons.

The category that makes sense, then, is a reasonable one inasmuch as people are able to bring to consciousness the various factors which influence concrete decisions. It is not, however, reasonable in the merely analytical sense, because persons do not experience the world in just that sense. Language about intuition has recently become popular again, but whatever term one uses—one might use instead aesthetic categories or categories based on affective responses, etc.—some attention must be placed on the kinds of human responses to the world which cannot be reduced to simply analytical reasoning. One of the reasons for the revival of the vocabulary of intuition and affectivities has been recent brain research which indicates that what we are calling analytical reasoning is characteristic of only half of the brain, the left side, and that data originating in the other half cannot be so well ordered. A lengthy examination of some of the components involved in weighing what makes sense can be found in Daniel Maguire's recent book *The Moral Choice.* Presumably a more sensitive psychology will gradually tell us even more about these mysteries and it is not my hope to try to describe them here.

But if reasonable in the context of moral decisions means bringing to consciousness a variety of factors some of which are not completely analyzable, what then is the usefulness of reason in moral matters? The answer lies partly in the tradition which associates moral reasoning with the ability to universalize one's behavior. The category 'universalizable' has been used to describe that factor of moral behavior which Kant noticed when he suggested that one criterion of the moralness of an action is that any other person of good will knowing all that this particular agent knows of the circumstances of his action would act in exactly the same way.[44] The position of such a moral consensus, the possibility that it makes sense to talk of human actions as universalizable, is an indication that even as we acknowledge that moral decisions cannot be analyzed in the same way as matters of fact can be analyzed, there is nevertheless a kind of consistency and reasonableness to them. But this reasonableness is elusive and it remains the case that the doing of ethics or the giving of moral advice is an appeal to the consciences of others and not simply a deductive matter.

The other side of universalizability most often remains only implicit in discussions such as these. If moral concern is natural to human beings, if human beings are everywhere the same, and if some features of the world remain the same, then it is possible to talk of learning about morality by observing what has worked for others in the past. It should also be possible to understand what features of the world or of the agents' experience explain actions once considered moral, but now no longer so considered. In other words, we can see that societies which, for example, encourage the old to die so that the young might be fed were not doing so out of a lack of moral sense, but that this seemed to be a behavior that made sense given the natural conditions of life.

The final claim that is implicit in the natural law tradition is that the working out of ordinary human reason is the way in which human beings can know what actions are pleasing to God. As a theological claim this one is outside of the province of this book but the claim should be noted as we turn to the last matters to be considered: the question of ultimacy and moral judgment.

FIVE

God, Morality, and Happiness

At the end of the preceding chapter we noted that specification of the principles of morality is not merely a matter of deductive reasoning; that the sense of the rightness of a moral practice is a more complicated judgment. Some of the larger implications of this complexity are worth looking at, as they go to the heart of the problems associated with the naturalness of morality. We have already suggested that the foundations of morality in reality could never be proven in the strictest sense, that natural morality falls under the same problems in this regard as does natural theology. It is no wonder, then, that the claims of morality are so vulnerable to the objections of both skepticism and, perhaps more surprisingly, mysticism.

One does not have to search far for an example of a skeptical attitude toward morality. Intellectual objections to the claims of morality are present in the philosophical literature of almost any era and the twentieth century is certainly no exception. H. L. A. Hart's attempt to reduce the claims of morality to those of survival, noted in the last chapter, is not even the strongest example to be found in recent times. The eighteenth-century Scot, David Hume, might stand as an example of the quintessential moral skeptic. Perhaps Hume's most famous contribution to modern ethics is in the following passage:

> In every system of morality, which I have hitherto met with, I have always remarked, that the author proceeds for some

> time in the ordinary way of reasoning, and establishes the being of a God, or makes observations concerning human affairs; when of a sudden I am surprised to find, that instead of the usual copulations of propositions, *is* and *is not,* I meet with no proposition that is not connected with an *ought* or an *ought not*. . . . As this *ought* or *ought not* expresses some new relation or affirmation, it is necessary that it should be explained; and at the same time that a reason should be given for what seems altogether inconceivable, how this new relation can be a deduction from others which are entirely different from it.[1]

This quotation is an important one, of course. The distinction between *is* statements and *ought* statements that Hume articulated so clearly has been one of the shibboleths of much twentieth-century moral philosophy. Hume was willing to extend his skepticism in all directions; so much so that he admitted that he found it impossible to live his skepticism. In a graceful passage he admits, "I dine, I play backgammon, I converse and am merry with my friends; and when, after three or four hours' amusement, I would return to these speculations, they appear so cold and strained and ridiculous that I cannot find in my heart to enter into them any further."[2] But whatever Hume's, or anyone's difficulty in living with skepticism, this position has received sufficient attention. The religious, or mystical, problems of natural morality, on the other hand, have not received the notice they deserve, and it is to these that we now turn.

Mysticism and Morality

Only recently has the relationship between mysticism and morality begun to receive scholarly attention, and the results have so far been inconclusive. Such discussion as has occurred has been fairly abstract and has tended to take Eastern mysticism as its focus.[3] The Christian version of the relationship between morality and mysticism seldom uses the latter word, preferring instead references to the 'will of God' or to 'divine commands'. The last phrase reminds us of Karl Barth, of course, who better than anyone else has stated the religious objection to natural law in our time. Religious objections to a notion of natural morality are well founded, although only up to a point. In fact, St. Thomas himself, that staunch proponent of natural law, saw its limitations from a religious point of view. It is worth examining his perspective on this in some detail.

In talking of the beginning of moral reasoning, we earlier made use of the notions of maintaining self-esteem and of doing 'what makes sense' in the conditions of one's life. These concepts are not St. Thomas', of course. He uses the category 'happiness'. The categories I have been using have some relationship to Thomas', but they by no means exhaust the nuances of 'happiness'. It is precisely the notion of happiness that we left out of our discussion of Thomas' first principle, and indeed the concept is a problematic one. Thomas uses the concept in the same double way he uses 'good' and, in fact, the two are synonyms for him. As we saw in Chapter Two, 'good' can mean 'that which is desirable' but it ultimately means God for Thomas. Likewise, 'happiness' can mean simply 'what all men desire' or it can mean man's last end, God. For Thomas, all human activity is the pursuit of happiness, and all activity that we call moral is a subset of that general human pursuit of happiness. The overarching generalization that is true of all human acts is that they are done in the pursuit of happiness. However many particular routes that man sees to this end, however complicated the relationship between this particular means and that end, men always act out of a belief that it would be better for them to act this way and not that. In this sense one of Thomas' uses of 'happiness'—as 'what all men desire'—is a truism. The difficulty lies not in this truistic sense of the word, but in giving content to the notion of happiness.

Pursuit of a particular notion of happiness makes it possible for us to make choices and to act; without some end in view we do not act deliberately at all. But if we are to gain any insight from these truisms as to how we should act, we shall have to be able to give some content to the notion of happiness. And there, of course, is a problem. The status of both 'good' and 'happiness' is problematic and, as we saw earlier, it is a problem clouded by a paradox:

> We can speak of the last end in two ways: first, considering only the aspect of last end; secondly, considering the thing in which the aspect of last end is realized. So, then, as to the

> aspect of the last end, all agree in desiring the last end: since all desire the fulfillment of their perfection, and it is precisely this fulfillment in which the last end consists . . . But as to the thing in which this aspect is realized, all men are not agreed, as to their last end: since some desire riches as their consummate good; some pleasure: others something else.[4]

Thomas accepts the fact that actual definitions of happiness run into problems, and he implicitly therefore accepts the notion that a particular definition of happiness is a matter of comparison and discussion, and not of evident truth. Indeed, the four questions which follow this passage are an examination of other notions of happiness and an explication of why Thomas holds the particular theory he does.

Such an admission that the nature of happiness is one on which humans can disagree is an important one, with considerable consequences for human morality. Thomas makes this point implicitly in a number of texts which span most of the years of his writing. He also makes it explicitly, as in the passage quoted above, or this one:

> Happiness can be considered in two ways. First according to the general notion of happiness: and thus, of necessity every man desires happiness. For . . . to desire happiness is nothing else than to desire that one's will be satisfied. And this everyone desires. Secondly we may speak of happiness according to its specific notion, as to that in which it consists. And thus all do not know happiness; because they know not in what thing the general notion of happiness is found.[5]

This point needs to be greatly stressed because the eighty questions of *Prima Secundae* which separate "On the Last End" from "On Law" tend to make it easy to forget that natural law is a way of talking about what happiness is, and Thomas' statements there are too often read as though he were claiming a certitude for all morals which he denies with respect to the keystone of his moral system: happiness.

Morals is for Thomas primarily the seeking of happiness. The meaning of happiness is defined in Thomas' view in relationship to human nature, the good for man is what he desires, but all things desire their own perfection.[6] Man's nature determines what his happiness is, and it is hard to see how man could have knowledge of one without also having knowledge of the other. I shall discuss later the sense in which Thomas does not think we know our own nature, but his repeated acknowledgment that we do not know what comprises our happiness is a reminder to us not to expect of Thomas more knowledge than is appropriate to us *in via.*

Thomas, of course, maintains that the vision of God is our true happiness, and that statement creates for him the paradox mentioned earlier with regard to 'good' and the way the rational appetite is moved. If God is our true happiness, then only he is a good great enough to move the will. Since in this world we lack a knowledge of God, it is a wonder that we can will at all. In view of this paradox, we seem now to have three different possible meanings of the concept of happiness:

1. As a definitional name for whatever moves the rational appetite.
2. True 'happiness', our true consummate good, is God himself and the enjoyment of the Beatific Vision. We cannot apprehend this good in this life without losing freedom of choice. Thomas clearly thinks we have such freedom and he has, in addition, theological reasons for maintaining that we do not apprehend God in this life.
3. False or less than adequate notions of happiness which move the wills of some and which seem to be necessary if we are to act volitionally in this world at all.

We have already seen that Thomas makes the distinction between the first analytic meaning of happiness and the subsequent synthetic ones. The distinction between the second and third is made in the *Summa* in various places, but nowhere so explicitly as in *The Trinity:*

> It must be said: the felicity of man is twofold. The one is imperfect felicity, which man may possess in this life, a felicity that the Philosopher speaks of, consisting in the knowledge of separated substances which man has by the virtue of wisdom. Yet this is imperfect, being only such knowledge or felicity as

> is possible on our journey as wayfarers, since the very essence of things, being itself, is unknown.
>
> Of another sort is that felicity by which, in heaven, God Himself will be made visible to us through His essence, and other separated substances will be known, but this will be a felicity attained, not through any of the sciences of speculations, but through the light of glory.[7]

This separation into wholly adequate and less than wholly adequate notions of happiness is analogous to the difference between eternal truth and human truth and, of course, to the parallel disjunction of eternal law and human law. But the problem seems more acute here, or rather here is where those theoretical distinctions become practical problems. Thomas seems much more concerned about this disjunction between perfect and imperfect happiness and mentions it more often and more explicitly than he does the others.

In order to see how Thomas handles this distinction of two kinds of happiness and what the status of the "less than adequate" notions are, we shall have to look at the way in which Thomas explains the epistemology of these two moves. One of the mysterious moments in human development is the transition from mimicking language to learning to use language intentionally. This is nowhere clearer than in the transition by which a child ceases to parrot the opinions of those who have taught him or her language and begins to make judgments of goodness on his or her own. The process is amazing enough if one is merely talking about the child's ability to make judgments about good apples; it is even more astounding when one speaks of the child's learning a moral sense of good. By comparison, the transition from 'good' to 'happiness' seems a relatively comprehensible one.

What Thomas may have in mind in making a transition from 'good' to 'happiness' is the process which is for him the ordinary way in which the mind forms concepts. From repeated instances of singulars the mind generalizes to form a universal. The latter term signifies for Thomas the generalization that the mind makes as a result of noting persisting similarities in experience. In his *Commentary on the Posterior Analytics* Thomas gives his own version of a statement of Aristotle's:

> . . . we consider this animal and that, e.g., man and horse until we arrive at some common animal, which is the genus. And in this we do the same until we arrive at some superior genus. Since therefore we attain the knowledge of universals from the singulars, he concludes that it is plain that it is necessary to the first universal principles to be known through induction. For thus, namely by way of induction, sense brings about the universal within the soul, inasmuch as all the singulars are considered.[8]

Thomas thus explicitly accepts this processs of generalizing to form universals as the way in which we come to form even the first universal principles. Even, that is, principles such as 'good is to be done . . .' are formed in this way, and so is the notion 'good'.

To form the universal 'good' the mind would note the resemblance between this thing I desire and that one, and so on as long as necessary until that which they have in common, desirability, would be recognized and it is that desirability which we call 'good'. That concept, however, would become a universal as we applied it to all of our desires, and from the process of desiring first this thing and then that, we would arrive at a concept of a good that would satisfy all of our desires and we call that 'happiness'. Thomas thus calls happiness 'a perfect and sufficient good'.[9]

We have here a process of generalization which is the common root of both Thomas' mysticism and moral skepticism. This notion of 'a perfect and sufficient good' is not one to which we can give any content. There is no logical way in which we could test out whether a given happiness was really a perfect and sufficient good. Thomas knows that this is so because such a good would have to be God himself, who is outside of the purview of our reason. Thus we can only make opaque references to true happiness like 'what satisfies all our desires' but we cannot have an adequate concept of what such a happiness is. This opacity is very similar to the opacity of the name *God.* Thomas would undoubtedly have argued that 'God is man's happiness' is one of those truths which would be analytically true from the standpoint of one who knew what 'God' or 'happiness' meant, but can be seen to be true by us only upon reflection. Even then the very fact that we need reflection indicates that we really don't know what the term means because the statement would still not be *per se nota* to us. Thomas uses this very example in discussing whether God's existence is self-evident:

> To know that God exists in a general and confused way is implanted in us by nature, inasmuch as God is man's beatitude. For man naturally desires happiness, and what is naturally desired by man must be naturally known by him. This however, is not to know absolutely that God exists; just as to know that someone is approaching is not the same as to know that Peter is approaching, even though it is Peter who is approaching; for many there are who imagine that man's perfect good which is happiness, consists in riches, and others in pleasures, and others in something else.[10]

If God is man's happiness, and if God is not known by us, then our happiness is not known by us. Rather, happiness is a state of affairs that we cannot imagine or describe, and because we cannot imagine or describe it, we cannot see how to make any connections between it and our present state of affairs. If all actions are moral or immoral according to whether or not they lead us toward or away from our last end, we cannot naturally know which, if any, actions are directed to our last end.

This is the path that leads to *mihi videtur ut palea* as well as to Hume's backgammon table. Thomas seems to have set up as necessary for human moral action a condition which cannot be fulfilled. If this were all that Thomas had said, his skepticism would have exactly equaled Hume's—for we would have no reason to act volitionally at all except the motivations provided by our senses, much less any way of discerning which actions are moral or not. Moralness or goodness is for Thomas measured primarily in a relationship—a relationship of means to end, and if we cannot know the end we cannot know the means to it. It is an indication of his awareness of this problem as well as a prelude to Thomas' solution to it to note his answer to the question "Can one know that he has charity":

> What a habit is, however, cannot be known unless one bases his judgment about it upon that to which that habit is ordained, which is the measure of that habit. But that to which

> charity is ordained cannot be comprehended, because its immediate object and end is God, the highest good, to whom charity unites us. Hence one cannot know from the act of love which he perceives within him whether he has reached the stage where he is united to God in the way which is needed for the nature of charity.[11]

This is the reason why questions of morals seem always open to question. It is always possible to question whether any given action is really a means to a given notion of happiness or to question whether any given notion of happiness is true happiness. The first question is more easily answered, but without a clear answer to the more problematic second one, our answer to the first is useless. If we do not know in what human happiness consists, how can we make judgments about what human beings ought to do? Or even if I know that my happiness consists in the vision of a God who is beyond this world, what steps within this world am I therefore enjoined to take as a means to that end? For Thomas, as well as for Hume, the standard by which the morality of actions is judged does not appear within our experience.

This is ultimately the theological core of Thomas' ethical writing, his belief that human happiness is in accord with human nature and that human nature leads us to seek our true happiness. His first principle of practical reason 'good is to be sought and done, evil is to be avoided' implies more than the recognition of what a desirable thing is and also more than a seeking after 'the good' or 'happiness' in the sense of a universal concept arrived at as a result of mental processes. 'Man has no choice but to desire happiness' is true for him not simply in the analytic sense already discussed but also in a synthetic sense that is too fragile for ordinary philosophic discourses as we know it. The good which men naturally seek is not the good of human languages, and even though all of us seek it we do not know what it is we are seeking. There is in Thomas a *via negativa* of the practical intellect as well as of the speculative one. He does not make an argument of the Kantian kind for the existence of God here, but his theory of man's moral nature is consistent with Kant's.

This is to say that, for Thomas, man's quest for happiness is inexplicable except in the context of man's desire for God, although it may be the case that a given man does not know that God is his happiness. What man experiences, according to Thomas, is a desire for happiness, or complete perfection; he does not experience God. To know that someone is approaching is not to know that Peter is approaching. But, for Thomas, the first principle of the practical intellect is to be fully understood not only in the way in which it was set out in the first part of Chapter Three, where we spoke of self-esteem maintenance, but also in this context. Although we mentioned in Chapter Four the contention of Hart and Sellars that moral duties can be spoken of only as a characteristic of persons as they exist in a community, and admitted that this contention can easily be fit into Thomas' scheme, we can see now why Thomas considers the source of the moral impulse to be even more deeply rooted in human nature. Thus, in Chapter Three, I included an imaginative picture of our contact with reality. One need not accept Thomas' contention that the desire for happiness impels man with the force he ascribes to it or that clues to this happiness are rooted in man's natural inclinations. The assurance Thomas has of their rightness is his Christian vision of a world in which nature does not fail in necessary things. But, on the other hand, these assumptions do not render Thomas' general theory religious rather than reasonable. Many general criticisms of Thomas arise from a failure to note these differences.

Thus, for example, D. J. O'Connor raises the following four criticisms:

> 1. The whole discussion seems to confuse two senses of "good" as (i) what *is* sought after and (ii) what *ought to be* sought after. What reason is there to suppose that there is any coincidence between happiness and virtue?
> 2. What reason is there to suppose that human beings have a characteristic function (ergon)? . . .
> 3. Granted that the good life for man must somehow be grounded in human nature, how do we argue from the *facts* of human nature to the *values* of morality?
> 4. Although the relation of means to ends does entail that some things are desired for their own sakes and not as a means to something else, we have no reason to suppose that there can be only *one* final end to which all our acts are

> means. Indeed our experience clearly shows that the ultimate objects of human desires and activities are many and diverse.[12]

Except for the third objection, which does not apply to Thomas' method of procedure, as we have seen, these are the right questions to ask. It is significant that O'Connor usually phrases the objections as questions and that where he does not, he should have. (What reason have we to believe that the *ultimate* objects of human desires and activities are many and diverse?) It might be argued, especially regarding the first objection, that there is no other way to proceed, but if there is any way of satisfactorily answering these questions, I do not know of it. Thomas may here be arguing from a religious assumption, but the whole point of the argument to which O'Connor's third objection refers is that he is not alone in thus proceeding.

All kinds of skepticism follow from this situation. The man who agrees with Thomas that God is man's last end can be skeptical about whether actions in this world lead to him, or can look to sources outside reason to direct our actions. The man who does not agree with Thomas that God is man's happiness but who thinks that man's happiness is unknowable is agreeing with the formal moves Thomas makes and is thus in a position that Thomas would understand. As I have already said, there is a close similarity between Thomas' mysticism and Hume's skepticism. There is a similarity, also, to the radical sense of human freedom and its accompanying anxiety, described by philosophers of the existentialist school.

The chief difference between Thomas and other philosophers who have seen through to this point is that Thomas seems to accept the limits of our knowledge more cheerfully than is typical. He has a belief that the world is created good by its maker and that our reason is enough to enable us to live in the world the way the creator intended. The status of humanity in this world, with its inevitable limitations, is accepted by Thomas as being the condition we find ourselves in as a result of the action of a beneficent god. He accepts the world and the necessity of living within it cheerfully, seeing divine providence where others see only inevitability. Whether this is the only world we have or the only one we have right now, the procedure is the same.

Thomas does not, however, say that actions in this world are connected in themselves to our happiness as means to an end. He says that with the proper intention and with the help of God our actions can be counted *as if* they were means to that end, but the connection is formed by our intention and not by the action itself. Thomas' name for this counting of our actions as if they were means to the end of perfect bliss is "merit" and the help of God is, of course, "grace" operating through charity.[13] In *de Veritate* he treats all of the practical reasons under the two categories *synderesis* and conscience as though the only criteria for rightness or wrongness of human acts was that we thought "in conscience" that we were acting rightly.[14] Granted, in talking thus of conscience he was implicitly talking about concern for the actions themselves and for their effects, but the omission is consistent with this side of Thomas' solution to the problem of happiness. For what the following of conscience means for Thomas is to follow the practical reason.[15] And what the natural law enjoins on us first of all is to follow reason.[16]

Another look at O'Connor's first objection can help us to proceed further, however. It is a metaphysical question about the congruence of virtue and happiness. In Thomas' system the two are defined in terms of one another so that what counts as virtue is the habit of acting in a way that is a means to attaining happiness. It thus is an analytic truth, in Thomas' system, that there is a coincidence between 'virtue' and 'happiness'. O'Connor's question however can be rephrased, "What reason is there to suppose that there is any coincidence between a particular notion of happiness and real happiness?"

For this question Thomas has two answers. First, not only is there no reason to suppose that there is any coincidence between a particular notion of happiness and real happiness, there is reason to think that *any* notion of happiness is false unless it is an opaque reference to the happiness of the blessed. There is, however, an assurance which arises from faith, either in Thomas' version or some other. This may be in keeping with reason, but it is beyond it. Secondly, however, and in spite of that limitation, we must accept the fact that the only way in which we can possibly act without self-contradiction is to do what *seems* right to us. That is, to act according to our reason. It may be that we are radically misled, but there is no other way to act.

Participation

Thomas goes further than this, I think. His belief is not simply that we are stuck with following our reasons whether or not it does us any good. He also believes that there is some relationship between our earthly notions of happiness and a kind of happiness which is at least partly adequate in this life. The notion of happiness which is the best that reason can do must have some relationship to our happiness *in via.* This, I think, is one meaning of his doctrine of participation in the natural law. The terminological confusion that we noted earlier with regard to these terms must now be sorted out.

Human beings are ruled by the law of God both in the sense that what we are is determined by the eternal law and in the sense that what we should do is known to us through our knowledge of what we are. Since law is for Thomas a dictate of reason, he calls the latter 'natural law', but it is logically and chronologically posterior to the former. What we know about natural law follows from what we know about our nature. The 'participation in the eternal law' is not an intuition for Thomas, it is a result of our knowledge of what we are, and what we are is determined by the eternal law. This has peculiar and perhaps not immediately evident results on our notion of happiness. It means that in some rough sense our notions of happiness are testable against our experience. The sense in which this is so is rough indeed, but extremely important. Secondly, and more obviously, it means that since whatever it means to be a human being is something we share with all other humans, certain features of our moral experience will remain constant in every time and every place. This second assertion amounts to the contention that what is usually called the 'natural law' does, in fact, exist in the sense given above. We shall have to look closely at this second result of participation in order to discover how much of natural law we can know.

The first result of participation is more difficult to understand or defend, although I think that it follows necessarily from the fact that we are ruled by the eternal law. It amounts to the assertion that not every logically possible system of morals will be experienced by human beings as productive of happiness. Since this notion of participation is the one for which there is least warrant in the text of Thomas (although Thomas thinks the natural law is "in infants . . . who cannot act by it"),[17] the fact that it amounts to simply saying that man has a determinate nature should be noted:

> The operation appropriate to a given being is a consequent of that nature. Now it is obvious that there is a determinate kind of nature for man. Therefore there must be some operations that are in themselves appropriate for man.[18]

This passage occurs as a prelude to a discussion of what man knows from the "natural order" of things, but the phrase 'natural law' does not occur. It is the side of this argument that Thomas does not pursue that I am concerned with here: not the knowledge of natural law but the *naturalness* of ethical systems. If man has a determinate nature, then some theoretically possible ethical systems are therefore humanly impossible, with 'impossible' here meaning that they would be experienced as producing not happiness but unhappiness.

It is one thing to make such a claim in general, without specification, and another to be clear about the ways in which an ethical code or a particular rule of conduct would be known to be unsatisfactory. In a way this specification is what Thomas believes is possible in speaking about 'natural law', but there is still a result of this belief of his which discussions of natural law do not ordinarily include. If the question is asked "How do we know that any particular notion of happiness resembles in any way real happiness?", Thomas' theory suggests the answer: try it and see. The boldness of that suggestion may be disquieting, but that it follows from Thomas' teaching seems to me to be unquestionable. In some ways the suggestion rests on a truism, that every language is adequate to the needs of its users, but to really expound and defend what seems to me to be clear implications of that truism and of Thomas' doctrine of participation might require a book-length study. That cannot be attempted here, but the point seems to me too important to be passed over lightly. I will attempt to sketch what is meant and to suggest a possible way of defending it philosophically.

A complete examination of this notion would include investigation of certain theories involved with the sociology of knowledge, philosophy of language, and such other fields related to them as anthropology and the history of science. I will use a model suggested by Thomas S. Kuhn in *The Structure of Scientific Revolutions.*[19] Kuhn's language is clearer and simpler than that of Peter Berger and Thomas Luckmann, whose *The Social Construction of Reality* sketches a theory of sociology of knowledge which is compatible with Kuhn's. The Berger-Luckmann book is more complete and more directly applicable to ethics, but Kuhn's simplicity will be useful in this brief exposition. Historians of science will have to judge the value of Kuhn's controversial work in his own field, but the model he suggests for the development of science and "normal science" seems to me to have clear analogies with what an elaboration of the facet of Thomas' natural law theory under discussion would look like.

Kuhn's central proposal develops from the concept of "normal science" and paradigm. " 'Normal science' means research firmly based upon one or more past scientific achievements that some particular scientific community acknowledges for a time as supplying the foundation for further practice."[20] This "achievement" he calls a paradigm and, although Kuhn does not use the phrase, it emerges in his discussion as a theoretical description of something in the world which explains a great many of the data which scientists have observed about that something but which they have not been able to account for in a coherent way. Perhaps the example easiest for a layman to grasp is that of Copernicus' theory of astronomy. The Ptolemaic system is as accurate, by today's standards, as that propounded originally by Copernicus, but as time had passed, the ability of the Ptolemaic system to serve as an explanation of what was observed to be going on in the movement of astronomical bodies had completely broken down. It was widely accepted that "no system as cumbersome and inaccurate as the Ptolemaic had become could possibly be true of nature."[21] The initial value of Copernicus' system was that it made sense where Ptolemy's did not—or appeared to do so. It was this ability to make sense of the data in a coherent way which led to its acceptance. Kuhn also has examples of the phlogiston theory of fire being replaced by the discovery of oxygen. The point of these examples is that a description of the world and what is in it breaks down if too many "counterfactuals" occur—that is, data that cannot be integrated into the general theory of what there is. In such a case a new paradigm, or model, is needed. It is the ability of a paradigm to convince scientists that it is capable of being expanded to fit all possible data, theoretically at least, that makes it accepted. While it is accepted it is normative in the sense that all "normal science" accepts the paradigm and works with it.

Kuhn points out that often the paradigm is not explicit:

> Though many scientists talk easily and well about the particular hypotheses that underlie a concrete piece of current research, they are little better than laymen at characterizing the established bases of their field, its legitimate problems and methods. If they have learned such abstractions at all, they show it mainly though their ability to do successful research.[22]

A paradigm is not to be confused with scientific rules or "laws" according to Kuhn. In some way the paradigm defines what there is—oxygen rather than phlogiston, a moving earth rather than a moving sun, etc.—while the rules define how "what there is" behaves. Rules can be added or subtracted without calling the paradigm into question, but the occurrence of data which cannot be integrated into the paradigm may, if the new data is plentiful enough or important enough, call the whole paradigm into question, and a situation of crisis occurs until a new paradigm is found. In a situation of normal science, the attention of researchers is directed to lacunae within the paradigm or to application of the paradigm to new cases.

Kuhn's analysis has been criticized because of the apparent falsifiability of certain scientific paradigms. He appears to maintain that scientific paradigms and laws are replaced with new paradigms because they lose their value as explanations and are replaced by what are perceived to be better explanations without having been disproven. That question aside, his framework seems ideally suited to philosophic explanations and to language about man used in the social sciences. There the impossibility of easy falsification of some theories is apparent in the very proliferation of theories. There the acceptance or rejection of a paradigm on the basis of explanatory power seems appropriate and suggestive.

The one point which interests us most in Kuhn's paradigm of how paradigms come to be and to function is the crisis situation and the reaction to it. Whatever the merits of Kuhn's theory as an explanation of the history and philosophy of science, it has interesting analogies, implicit and explicit in our reading of Thomas' theory of the way ethics works. A functioning paradigm seems to be a synthetic *a priori,* or an interrelated set of such statements, of a given community. Since the notion of *per se nota* truth in Thomas has great similarity to the notion of synthetic *a priori,* this aspect of Thomas' thought can help us to see the similarities between what he is saying and what Kuhn is saying.

As we saw in Chapter Four, Thomas' discussion of how the "fixed principles of knowledge" are arrived at is remarkably similar to Wilfred Sellar's discussion of the status of statements true *ex vi terminorum.* Sellars, like Thomas, believes that any system of language that can be used to make fixed references to experience needs to have some fixed elements in it.[23] Like Thomas he believes that these arise in experience. The difference between the two is that for Sellars the "unconditionally assertable" quality of such statements is conferred by the syntactical rules of the language, whereas Thomas speaks of its being "conferred by the mind," but clearly their meaning is quite close. The differences between the two are not great, and a case can be made for saying that the two are quite compatible.[24] Without modifying the language of the two to bring them into line, it can still be noticed that both accept the possibility that such *ex vi terminorum* truths can be modified: Sellars explicitly, Thomas more implicitly. Thomas' example ("this drug cures fever") seems to indicate that should a significant number of cases arise where the drug does not cure the fever, then the unconditionally assertable statement concerning the drug would no longer be unconditionally assertable and a new principle of science would have to be found. In both cases a statement once considered true on the basis of experience has become, by repeated confirmation, a fixed truth. In this sense the statement is both synthetic and unconditionally assertable and Sellars is willing to call it a *synthetic a priori.* He points out, however, that he is using that term only with the understanding that such statements are unconditionally assertable only as long as they are useful—as long as they work.

This example, however, does not correspond to what Kuhn refers to as a paradigm; it is a rule of a given paradigm rather than a paradigm itself. In Sellars' proposal, the entire conceptual system would be a kind of master paradigm composed of an interrelated system of lesser paradigms, each of which defined what there is in a particular aspect of reality. Sellars explicitly states that his synthetic *a priori* statements function within a system and refer to "primitive descriptive predicates," but he is equally explicit about the importance of the whole conceptual system and, by extension the "families" or "games" within it. The interesting analogy with Kuhn lies in the fact that when a previously accepted rule ceases to function as unconditionally assertable, correction may lie in the direction of applying our given conceptual system more rigorously to experience or, if the damage to the system is too great, by changing the system.

> Not only can we be *caused* to modify our linguistic frame, we can deliberately modify it—teach ourselves new habits—and give reasons for doing so.[25]

This excursion into paradigms and conceptual systems is important not because Thomas says very nearly the same thing as Sellars and Kuhn, but because his theory of participation has direct relevance to the particular paradigm or conceptual scheme which is moral language. The language of paradigms may be unfamiliar in this context, but if we think of a paradigm of what happiness is or of what equality is, the meaning becomes clearer. There would obviously be a number of such paradigms in a moral system. If Thomas is correct, the two consequences of participation mentioned above will have great bearing on a paradigm of morality or a conceptual structure of moral language. First, there will be certain true statements found in all moral paradigms—and this is what Thomas' statements about natural law are all about. Secondly, in the long run only paradigms which are adequate to human nature will work. In a sense Thomas spells out in his primary precepts what paradigms are needed without giving a paradigm.

The statement that any system of morals or moral scheme—and I use these terms as equivalent to 'paradigm of morality' and 'conceptual structure of moral language'—would, if it is going to work, have to be adequate to human nature is equivalent to saying that any conceptual scheme which is concerned with things in the world would have to be, in some measure at least, adequate to the nature of the world.

The analogy I wish to draw from this discussion is first of all the need that the paradigm explain all the data or, at least, that it be believed capable of explaining all the data. In Thomas' notion of participation in eternal law there are basic human needs which must be accounted for and the awareness of these basic human needs is the data to which moral paradigms must conform. He believes that persons know when paradigms are adequate or not in much the same way that Kuhn would explain how an adequate paradigm is recognized. Once a paradigm has become a paradigm, once it is embedded in the language so firmly that it is taken to be self-evidently true, it can be changed only with a great deal of trouble, if at all. It is not changing them which is Thomas' interest, however. If we remember that Sellars' term *ex vi terminorum* is closely related to Thomas' term *per se nota,* we note that Thomas thinks that *per se nota* statements are true but also that only statements which are true to man's experience of himself can become *per se nota.*

Thomas believes that any system of truths which are *per se nota* are true, but he also seems to believe that only one set of such truths can exist. It is not a great extension of this thought, however, to say that another such set of truths, if they are genuinely perceived to be *per se nota,* would be equally as valid. Thomas may have believed that only one such set could be perceived as true but his reasons for believing this are such that he would be forced to accept another set *so long as they met his criterion.*

This notion of adequacy, although it seems to be true, is problematic. We cannot adopt a neutral viewpoint and put our language about the world next to the world and see what is the relationship between them. God can do that, but we can't. Theories of analogy attempt to describe that relationship, but they are only attempts.

There is no way in which we can compare our language about the world with the way the world really is. In Thomas' vocabulary this is so because of the contrast, spoken of earlier, between eternal truth and human truth. The source of all difficulties in talking about analogy in Thomas is that the relationship between the two is not clear. But there is a sense, both in Thomas' theory and linguistic philosophy, in which it is necessary to assume a rough correlation between the world and our language about the world. This is simply to say that the value of our human language is that it enables us to communicate with one another and to make references to the world around us which can be the basis of prediction, action and the like. If discrepancies between our language and the world get too great, the language ceases to perform its function and must be changed; in ordinary cases added to or subtracted from: 'oxygen' is added, 'phlogiston' disappears. Although we cannot predict how or when, our ability to use language referentially at all depends on its correspondence with the world. It also seems that the less empirically observable the reference of a word is, the more susceptible is it to undergoing change.

My point here is not such that we need to get too involved in the matter of how languages change, but that it is a presupposition of our using language to refer to things at all that language about the world and the world itself somehow correspond. There is no reason to suppose that this rough correspondence stops short of ourselves and the ways in which we talk about ourselves. In other words, if we assume that the world remains the same there must be some elements in our language about ourselves which are constant and some thoughts about ourselves which just won't work. In some way what we are must act as a standard for what we can possibly think we are. Presumably, also, language about our needs and desires must somehow also be conformed to our real needs and desires; moral language must work in some way or it cannot retain its usefulness.

I am not suggesting that we can examine our natures and see whether our moral language conforms to it. Nor that we can, as a result of our own or a larger community's experience, generalize as to what exactly a moral system must look like if it is to work. I am saying only that there must be some limits to what such a system would be like and that, although we could not tell in advance what those limits are, it would be clear to us in practice if something were going wrong.

This proposal does not rest on the assumption that man has a 'nature' in the sense that it assumes that all men are everywhere and in every time exactly the same. Although Thomas does indeed think this, the notion of testability I am suggesting could easily make room for several different kinds of human natures over a broad spectrum. But to the extent that language about morals is public language, enough community of experience is presupposed to make communication possible. Thus some kind of community of natures is presupposed, although its limits suggest themselves readily.

An example may be useful. It is one of the scenarios of the future that is often repeated that someday human children will be produced in test tubes, that is, in laboratories—rather than inside a woman's body.[26] On the face of it, for reasons we have not examined, Thomas would probably have declared such a possibility contrary to nature. However, assuming that it were to become scientifically possible (which at present seems incredible), the test of whether or not it was contrary to nature would be theoretically possible. If it were, then the effects of such a practice would be recognized as wrong. Assuming the present institutions of society, several things might occur. The parents might react in a way which makes the method unsatisfactory. The offspring might be recognizably too different, psychologically or physiologically, to be integrated into society. The children themselves, when matured, might feel that the process was unsatisfactory. If such good reasons did not occur, after the fact, then there would be no reason to condemn the project.

But, to go a step further, suppose that the reasons the project did not work were seen as being the psychological conditioning of the parents and these were not considered good enough reasons to stop the project. The enterprise then would have to include changing the institution of parenthood. It could be said that the new method of producing children did not work in the old paradigm of parenthood, but that the whole paradigm had to be changed. This change would then fall under the same trial and error testing of the previous, more limited change. And so on.

The process sounds exceedingly flexible and pragmatic, but the difficulties involved should not be overlooked. One of the consequences of what this book has been arguing is that human beings are recognizably the same, in different times as well as in different places. One of the functions of "the wise," for Thomas—a function fulfilled today by those whom we call moralists or ethicists—is to learn from the past experience of human beings. And it seems clear to me that the example I have chosen is beyond our powers of adaptation, at least at the present time (and in general). Changing notions of what light is may produce scientific 'revolutions' but such revolutions involve little danger to the welfare of human beings. Changing the institutions of society, however, is obviously a much different situation, one laden with great potentiality for harm for human welfare. The appearance of flexibility may, indeed, turn out to be entirely deceiving. Perhaps with this institution the limits of human adaptability are so narrow that no change will be possible. The kind of argument the example presupposes is one that could be called psychological or anthropological. Such is obviously the line of argument that a developed notion of participation presupposes.[27]

Thomas, when he speaks of participation in the eternal law, generally refers to our awareness of this participation rather than the participation itself. But his argument about how we come to be aware of "natural law" as a result of "natural inclinations" is obviously designed to show that this awareness follows on experience and does not presuppose an intuition on the part of man. His discussion of natural law then appears to be a discussion of the permanent elements of any system of ethics that works.

The phrase 'system of ethics that works' reiterates a problem. The importance of the whole system, rather than individual parts of it must be stressed. If we were to take 'science' as a master paradigm we would expect all of the various paradigms which constitute it to bear 'family resemblances' such that the various paradigms were at least theoretically compatible with one another. Likewise, taking practical discourse as a master paradigm we would expect all of the various paradigms which comprise it to be at least theoretically compatible. I will contend that the integrating factor in the latter is a notion of what man is, and that this root notion connects the various paradigms of marriage, justice, equality, etc. In talking about systems that work we should emphasize this theoretical unity of the system because Thomas' classification of 'good' as a 'transcendental' indicates that its meaning cannot be defined within a given language—within human truth—but can only be understood as applying to the whole system and its fulfilling of human needs.

This explanation of the primary meaning of participation and its implications for Thomas has led us in the direction of an explanation of where Thomas gets a notion of happiness. We will have to complete the journey before looking at the other half of participation—our knowledge of it, natural law.

Earlier we noted that one way in which we could move from the initial concept 'good' which means desirable to a concept 'happiness' or 'good for human beings' is by way of the reason's forming a notion of universal good. That procedure leads to a blank wall and the realization that it does so can lead either to the identification of happiness with God or to moral skepticism. That point is an important one and needs to be made, but the procedure by which we arrive at the concept 'happiness' should now be reexamined, for the impression earlier given that the mind *first* conceives of happiness as unimaginable absolute and then turns to the practical reason as the next best thing is not correct.

Thomas gives us the impression that after we realize that we must live in this world, we must then turn to our reason and fabricate a moral system and a concept of happiness. In reality, however, beginning by looking at our impulses is probably the opposite order to what actually takes placd. In coming to use our reasons we come to learn a particular language and to live in a particular culture. Thomas is not as aware of this fact as we are, although, as we shall see, he makes allowance for this fact in what he teaches. We will proceed with our investigation and return to Thomas' awareness of diversity of cultures when we speak of primary and secondary precepts of the natural law.

Thomas believes that happiness is the perfection of what man is. All things seek their perfection and the explanation of desire for Thomas is the movement of all things to make themselves perfect. The correlation of what man is and what his happiness is is therefore clear. It is also clear that evaluations both of what man is and of what happiness is are what Kuhn would call paradigms in the sense that they are already built into rules and practices of a language and culture and that they are explanations of what there is. (I am using 'language' to mean not only linguistic rules and behavior but also all of the cultural rules and practices which one learns together with language.) This is clearly the case for Thomas, for any moral choice is made with an end in view and the existence of a moral rule means the existence of a notion of the end in view.

Earlier we noted that the way in which the mind forms a notion of "happiness" is to generalize out of the experience of 'goods' a notion of 'the good' for man. But an individual does not begin this process with only the patterns of stimulus/response of the sensitive appetite. The 'material' from which the mind generalizes is a particular set of patterns and linguistic procedures—the rules of a particular language. From which it follows that the first notions of happiness and of what it means to be human that the mind arrives at are the ones which are already embedded in the language that one learns. In his discussions of teaching Thomas makes exactly this point, saying that the teacher does not begin by teaching the student the first principles but by showing him the conclusions and reasoning backward to the first principle:

> The teacher proposes some things, the principle of which the pupil does not understand when first taught, but will know later when he has made some progress in the science.[28]

Thomas is in the habit of talking as though we learned deductively when, as a matter of fact, he believes we learn initially by induction and justify by deduction. His category *per se nota to the wise* is interesting and instructive in this regard. The connection between what a human is and a given understanding of, say, prudence, is not made explicitly in the learned language, but can be inferred, upon reflection by the wise. An adequate defense of this point would be a discussion of the existence of 'brute facts', and related philosophical issues. There seems little question, however, that such values are transmitted in language itself and this point about transmission is sufficient for our purposes.

This is the heart and soul of one branch of the 'is/ought' problem: not that we begin by learning 'is statements' and then somehow must get to 'ought statements'—we learn both at the same time and in the same way. More, in some sense, some of our 'is statements' are 'ought statements' at the same time. We do not, for example, learn what the institution of promising is and then decide whether we should keep our promises. We learn 'one ought to keep his promises' as we learn what promising is. Similarly we do not learn that we are different from horses and other animals simply on the basis of who rides whom, but we learn that, in countless ways, we ought to act differently. It is from this kind of data that we learn a paradigm of what a human being is and this paradigm consists of both 'is judgments' and 'ought judgments', and the two are inseparably related. It is from the paradigm of *what a human being is* that we generate a notion of *what a human being ought to be* if he is to be happy, or rather these are already outlined for us in the culture.

When Thomas talks of right reason we may sometimes hear the implication that there is a higher reason than that which we ordinarily possess. But human reason must inevitably be exercised within this world and that means within a paradigm, for it is only within a paradigm that we can determine what ends we should seek. His paradox is resolved by the fact that we find ourselves within a language system and can speak of acting for an end within the system and saying that the whole system is orientated toward the ultimate end of man. It is by acting rightly or wrongly within the system that we merit eternal life.

We are in a position now to examine the initial moves by which Thomas brought us into the language of *what we ought to do.* We said then that it was impossible to say definitely that Thomas had introduced a moral sense of 'ought' into the practical reason, because we had not yet a notion of what happiness is. With the entrance into a language that is both descriptive and evaluative we are able to see that Thomas can indeed say that we learn that "good is to be done" in a moral sense.

The notion of good or happiness that one first finds in a language system is the one he first learns to use; it is on a continuum from his first use of 'good' as satisfying desire. Generalizing from that first use of 'good' leads the mind eventually to use the word 'good' in the sense in which things and actions are called good in the society. Moreover, he finds that he must abide by the rules of the society if he is to live in peace in the society, and identifies it as being in his best interest to follow the rules of the society. But more than that, he finds himself taught a particular notion embedded in the institutions of the society.

Within a given society there may be differing notions of what man is and what would make him happy, of course, but these will not be of such kind that they are completely unintelligible to one another, or a situation of great social instability results.

The question might then be asked why a particular individual internalizes or appropriates for himself a particular notion of happiness, especially when such an internalization involves him in situations where the benefits to the agent are not immediately clear. What reason can be given for entering the community of discourse where good is spoken of, or for seeking after happiness? That is, why bother with happiness at all? The implicit answer is that we must simply accept the fact that we seek after happiness—just as, in the vocabulary used earlier, we seek to maintain our self-esteem. Thomas has an explanation of why we seek happiness, but one can disagree with his explanation and still not have disproved the fact. The choice is to act or not to act, but since in fact we all act, we all have, in Thomas' terms, chosen *goods.* We may have chosen badly, but we have chosen.

Part of what Thomas means by participation in the natural law can be extended to include the assurance that these notions are self-correcting. That is, a paradigm which did not adequately meet what Thomas calls "natural inclinations" would be too unstable to last—but we are talking in "the long run." To say this one need not be unaware that what appear to be bad paradigms can last a long time: polygamy, for example. There seem to be two possible answers to this observation. One is that if it does not appear to the people who live within it to be a bad paradigm, then it is not one. A more persuasive explanation might be the fact of human sinfulness. A situation where a given practice does not arise out of consensus but is forced on a group as a result of power, for example, would be such a situation.

Conclusion

Our concern in this essay has been to present a version of the natural law tradition that is open to historical change and development and is yet true to the central insights of an outstanding spokesman of that tradition, Thomas Aquinas. The picture of natural law that emerges is one that places the human need to be good in the ordinary experience of human beings. More, it also specifies, in a general way, the areas of human life which are the ones in which human beings experience the desire to be good. It leaves unspecified, however, the concrete institutions and practices in these areas which would be the determination of persons in particular circumstances. At a high enough level of generality some of these judgments are indeed without exception: Thomas as we have seen, uses as an example "do evil to no man." Or, to make the same point, we may prefer the more symbolic language of the virtues: justice, for example, is to treat other persons appropriately, i.e., in a good manner. This high level of generality, with the accompanying need for specification according to the historical situation, is enough for our purposes. My intention has been to establish the real basis of morality which is the cornerstone of the natural law tradition and to make possible an understanding of that tradition which is consonant with the changes which time and place necessitate.

Some readers may find in the foregoing only a justification for moral relativism. I have argued, it is true, that the specific conventions of morality—the ways in which fundamental insights into what it means to be a human being in the world—may vary from place to place and from time to time. In doing so I have said no more than Thomas Aquinas, but Thomas went on to add his long volume about specific virtues to his short "Treatise on Law"—and this book stops far short of such comprehensiveness. To emphasize the relativity of human moral conventions, however, is to miss most of the thrust of this essay. The other side of what I have been arguing has been that in all of our moral judgments—individual as well as communal—we are deciding about reality, because human moral judgment is in touch with reality. This latter statement is fundamental to the natural law tradition and nothing in this book contradicts it.

At the level of naturalistic consequences the real basis of morality is apparent only in the long run, and especially when looking at whole communities rather than individuals. (But even for the individual it is true that we carry the consequences of our actions with us, as the psychologists tell us.) This perspective of 'the long run' makes the relationship of act and consequences hard to pin down, but history seems to bear out the generalization, and perhaps the other social sciences may someday make the relationship clearer. At the level not of actions but of motivations, the relationship of morality and reality is even less clear, as the last chapter has indicated. In this sphere we find the possibility of human freedom, the likelihood of self-delusion, the mystery of what it means to be a human being, and, perhaps, the presence of God.

In stable communities it is possible to make the moves of morality with ease—it is a necessity of stability that a moral consensus exist on fundamental issues. In unstable ones such moves are more difficult and it is possible to even suppose that moral consensus is unnecessary. Perhaps our times will provide us with an unwelcome opportunity to see whether this is the case. Whether consensus exists or not, however, moral appeals are always appeals to conscience. We may wish we knew more clearly what it is to be a human being in this world, we may wish moral appeals to nature could be demonstrated more easily; but our sense of these things is a fragile one and our ability to interpret or respond to the demands of conscience is equally fragile.

Notes

Chapter One

1. An excellent review of recent literature on the subject of natural law is provided in Michael B. Crowe, "The Pursuit of Natural Law," *Irish Theological Quarterly,* Vol. 44 (1977), 3–29. The classic review of the history of the tradition remains A. P. D'Entrevres' *Natural Law* (London: Hutchinson, 1951; revised edition Atlantic Highlands, N.J.: Humanities, 1964).

2. *Principia Ethica* (Cambridge: Cambridge University Press, first edition 1903; paperback edition 1959). Moore's position is frequently associated with that taken by David Hume at the end of Book III, Part 1, Section 1, of his *Treatise of Human Nature* usually called the is/ought problem, *viz.,* that there is no way to logically infer from a statement of fact ("is") any kind of moral conduct ("ought"). The literature on these two positions is enormous. Although not all philosophers paid attention to these assertions, among those who did four possibilities have been explored: 1) that moral language was "meaningless," cf. A. J. Ayer, *Language, Truth and Logic* (London: Gollancz, 1935; paperback edition New York: Dover, no date); 2) that moral statements were to be identified with some subjective reaction such as emotion, cf. Charles L. Stevenson, *Ethics and Language* (New Haven: Yale University Press, 1944); 3) that it is possible to find some way around them, cf. John R. Searle, "How to Derive Ought From Is," *Philosophical Review,* Vol. 73 (1964), 43–58; and 4) that one may defend the reasonableness of morals in spite of Moore's and Hume's points; examples of this are given in the text.

3. Cf. Moore, *op. cit.,* p. 40. I return to this topic in Chapter Three.

4. Francesco Cardinal Roberti, *et. al., Dictionary of Moral Theology,* trans. Henry J. Yannone, *et. al.* (Westminster: Newman, 1962), p. 697.

5. *We Hold These Truths* (New York: Sheed and Ward, 1960; paperback edition, Garden City: Doubleday, 1964), p. 280. All citations are from the paperback edition.

6. (Cambridge, Mass., 1971).

7. William K. Frankena, *Perspectives on Morality,* ed. K. E. Goodpaster (Notre Dame: University of Notre Dame Press, 1976), p. 37.

8. *The Moral Choice* (Garden City: Doubleday, 1978), pp. 72–73.

9. *Op. cit.,* pp. 316–17. Murray does not use the word 'historicity'.

10. A good summary of the meanings of the word 'law', including several not mentioned here, can be found in Frederick S. Carney, "Outline for a Natural Law Procedure for Christian Ethics," *Journal of Religion,* vol. 47 (1967), 28–31.

11. Albert Camus, *The Myth of Sisyphus,* trans. Justin O'Brien (New York: Random House, 1955), p. 137.

12. *Op cit.,* p. 316.

13. Quoted in *The Many-Faced Argument,* ed. John Hick and Arthur C. McGill (New York: Macmillan, 1967), pp. 216–17.

14. Relevant titles include e.g., Brown, *Love's Body* (New York: Random House, 1966); Rieff, "The Impossible Culture," *Encounter* (Sept., 1970), 33–44; Lifton, *The Life of the Self* (New York: Simon and Schuster, 1976); Hillman, "The Fiction of Case History: A Round," in *Religion as Story,* ed. James B. Wiggins (New York: Harper & Row, 1975). A fuller list of authors relevant to the matter is given in Lifton, p. 17.

15. (New York: The Free Press, 1973; paperback edition 1975). Becker has been sharply criticised by Donald Evans for promoting narcissism, cf. his review of *The Denial of Death, Religious Studies Review,* vol. 5, No. 1 (January, 1979), 25–34.

16. This section is adapted from my article "St. Anselm in the Social Science Quad: The Ontological Argument One More Time," *Horizons,* Vol. 7 (1980).

Chapter Two

1. The reading of St. Thomas in this chapter is amply supported by his writings. I wish to emphasize, however, that the purpose of this chapter is not directly concerned with thirteenth-century theology or with historical studies of Thomas Aquinas. The procedure I am following has been defended as "Revisionism" by David Tracy: cf. *Blessed Rage For Order* (New York: The Seabury Press, 1975).

2. The work of thinkers such as these has been ignored in modern scholarship. Even D'Entrevres, *op. cit.* ignores them, yet they were extremely important in Catholic thought for centuries.

3. Sturm traces the idea back to Karl Mannheim. See "The Meaning of Citizenship: An Exercise in Constructive Political Theory" in *Belief and Ethics,* ed. W. Widick Schroeder and Gibson Winter (Chicago: Center for the Scientific Study of Religion, 1978), esp. pp. 258–60.

4. Cf. Newman's *Development of Christian Doctrine* (Westminster: Christian Classics, 1968).

5. I shall refer to *Quaestiones Disputatae de Veritate* by this title. The Latin text of Thomas has been consulted (Romae: ex typographia polyglotta S.C. de propaganda fide, 1882–1906). In general, available English translations have been used and are cited. Standard citations are used. Where my own translation is used, reasons are given.

6. Hereafter referred to as *Commentum.*

7. Cf. Victor S. Preller, *Divine Science and the Science of God: A Reformulation of Thomas Aquinas* (Princeton: Princeton University Press, 1967).

8. *Commentum,* I, VII, 1, 1. Translation is from Preller, p. 271.

9. *A Man For All Seasons* (New York: Random House, 1962).

10. Cf, John S. Dunne, "St. Thomas' Theology of Participation," *Theological Studies,* vol. XVIII (1957), 475ff.

11. Cf. Anthony Battaglia, *op. cit.*

12. Translations from *de Veritate* are from *Truth,* 3 vols., trans. Robert W. Mulligan, James V. McGlynn, S.J., and Robert W. Schmidt, S.J. (Chicago: Henry Regnery Co., 1952–54).

13. 'Analogy' is a very flexible category and has been interpreted by different authors in very different ways. Compare, e.g., Preller's treatment (*op. cit.,* pp. 168–69) with that of James F. Ross, "Analogy as a Rule of Meaning for Religious Language," in *Aquinas: A Collection of Critical Essays,* ed. Anthony Kenny (Garden City: Doubleday, 1969).

14. *Summa Theologiae* I-II, Q.91, A.1. Translations from the "Treatise on Law" (I-II, QQ.90–97) are from the Blackfriars edition (New York: McGraw-Hill, 1966). This volume is translated by Thomas Gilby, O.P. *The Summa Theologiae* will hereafter by referred to in the text as *Summa* and in notes as *S.T.*

15. Note that Thomas' use of the term law implies from God's point of view an analogy to civil law, while from the human point of view it implies an analogy to scientific law or a 'law of nature'.

16. *S.T.,* I, Q.15, A.1.

17. *de Veritate,* Q.1, A.1.

18. *Ibid.,* Q.1, A.4.

19. *S.T.,* Q.87, A.1.

20. For Thomas, such a situation would mean that, for us, the word truth would have no meaning. Obviously, if we can use our 'truth' to get

around in the world, there must be some correlation between the two.

21. *de Veritate,* Q.8, A.16, reply.

22. *Ibid.,* Q.8, A.17.

23. In *The Silence of St. Thomas,* trans. John Murray, S.J. and Daniel O'Connor (Chicago: Henry Regnery Co., 1957).

24. Preller, *passim.*

25. *S.T.,* I, Q.16, A.2.

26. Preller, p. 78.

27. Cf. Note 13, above.

28. *S.T.,* I, Q.84, A.5. Except for the "Treatise on Law," quotations from *S.T.* are from that of the Dominican Fathers (New York: Benziger Bros., 1947).

29. *S.T.,* I-II, Q.91, A.2.

30. *de Veritate,* Q.1, A.2.

31. *S.T.,* I, Q.87, A.1. Using this formulation we might say that while God knows the truth of things (their essences) we know only the truth of the appearance of things. Formally, what God knows *is* eternal truth as it "resides" in creation.

32. *S.T.,* I-II, Q.94, A.2.

33. *S.T.,* I, Q.79, A.12.

34. *S.T.,* I, Q.84, A.5.

35. *S.T.,* I-II, Q.94, A.1.

36. *S.T.,* I-II, Q.100, A.4.

37. *S.T.,* I-II, Q.94, A.2.

38. I return to this point later in this chapter.

39. *de Veritate,* Q.16, A.1.

40. Cf. Germain Grisez, "The First Principle of Practical Reason," in *Aquinas: A Collection of Critical Essays,* ed. Anthony Kenny (Garden City: Doubleday, 1969).

41. The placing of precepts of natural law is a troublesome one. As known by practical reason they belong in the next category, but as "natural inclinations" (their subject matter) they stand outside of both *synderesis* and practical reason. It is in acknowledgement of their pre-rational character that I place them here.

42. Available in English trans. The Dominican Fathers (New York: Benziger Bros., 1947).

43. *Commentum,* Dist. 35, Q.4, A.4; *Supplementum* Q.65, A.1. Italics mine.

44. *Supplementum,* Q.49, A.3.

45. *Supplementum,* Q.65, A.3.

46. *Ibid.*

47. *Summa Contra Gentiles,* III, 129. English translation by Vernon J. Bourke (Garden City: Doubleday, 1956).
48. *S.T.* I-II, QQ.1–5, especially Q.3, A.8; cf. also *S.T.* I, Q.6.
49. *S.T.,* I, Q.80, A.1.
50. *Ibid.*
51. *S.T.,* I, Q.82, A.2., ad 3.
52. *S.T.,* I, Q.82, A.2, ad 2.
53. *S.T.,* I, Q.82, A.3.
54. *S.T.,* I-II, Q.1, A.2.

Chapter Three

1. *S.T.,* I-II, Q.94, A.2
2. Among recent Christian objections to natural law, the preeminent one is that of Karl Barth; cf. *Church Dogmatics,* vol. III, no. 4, section 52, English edition trans. A. T. Mackay, *et. al.* (Edinburgh: T. & T. Clark, 1961), pp. 3–46.
3. A concise discussion of psychological egoism can be found in William K. Frankena, *Ethics,* second edition (Englewood Cliffs, N.J.: Prentice-Hall, 1973), pp. 20–23.
4. Awareness of death has recently become a fashionable topic. The primary philosophical source for a discussion of its human importance remains Martin Heidegger, *Being and Time,* trans. John Macquarrie and Edward Robinson (New York: Harper & Row, 1962). The following discussion pursues the topic not in the language of Heidegger but in the more accessible terminology of some recent humanistic social scientists; cf. Ernest Becker, *The Denial of Death* (New York, Macmillan, 1973; paperback 1975) and Robert Jay Lifton (New York: Simon and Schuster, 1976), cited above, Chapter Two, Note 14.
5. *The Structure of Evil* (New York: George Braziller, 1968; paperback edition New York: Macmillan, 1976), pp. 327–46. Becker argues that self-esteem is "the single unifying principle" of "the science of man." Becker's analysis, here and in *The Denial of Death* is marred by too rigid a separation between the physical and the mental, which leads him to sometimes deny the reality of anything but the physical; cf. Donald Evans "Review of *The Denial of Death,*" *Religious Studies Review,* vol. 5, no. 1 (January 1979), pp. 25–34.
6. For Thomas, all human acts are moral or immoral; he denies the possibility of an "indifferent" deliberate act. *S.T.,* I-II, Q.18, A.9. For a somewhat more restricted notion of the moral that is nevertheless akin to Thomas' position, cf. W. D. Falk, "Morality, Self and Others" in *Morality and the Language of Conduct,* ed. Hector-Neri Castaneda and George Nakhnikian (Detroit: Wayne State University Press, 1965), pp. 25–67.

7. A great deal of psychological research into moral development has been done by L. Kohlberg; cf. his *Collected Papers on Moral Development and Moral Education* (Cambridge, Mass.: Moral Education and Research Foundation, 1973).

8. One recent defender of a naturalism something like the one I am proposing has been Philippa Foot; cf., e.g., her "Moral Beliefs," *Proceedings of the Aristotelian Society,* vol. 59 (1958–59), pp. 83–104.

9. "Unwise and Untimely?" (Nyack, New York: Fellowship of Reconciliation, no date), pp. 7–8, reprinted in *Ways of Being Religious,* ed. Frederick J. Streng, *et. al.* (Englewood Cliffs, N.J.: Prentice-Hall, 1973), pp. 199–200.

10. William K. Frankena discusses this notion of morality, and argues against it in "The Concept of Morality," *The Journal of Philosophy,* vol. 63 (1966), pp. 125–32.

11. But such an assumption does seem to be common in much psychological theory: cf. Philip Rieff, *The Triumph of the Therapeutic* (New York: Harper & Row, 1966). Rieff himself argues against this position in "The Impossible Culture," *Encounter,* September 1970, 33–44. Another statement in line with my argument is that of Martin Buber in "Guilt and Guilt Feelings," *The Knowledge of Man,* ed. Maurice Friedman (New York: Harper & Row, 1966).

12. This statement is a paraphrase of one he makes in the preface to *The Sickness Unto Death,* trans. Walter Lowrie (Princeton: Princeton University Press, 1941; paperback edition Garden City: Doubleday, 1954), p. 142. In this passage Kierkegaard is specifically talking of "Christian heroism" but the passage reflects similar statements made of humans in general in *Concluding Unscientific Postscript,* trans. David F. Swenson and Walter Lowrie (Princeton: Princeton University Press, 1969), pp. 217–221.

13. *Morality and Beyond* (New York: Harper & Row, 1963; paperback edition 1966), p. 20.

14. *S.T.*, I-II, Q.94, A.2.

15. The model of this 'thought-experiment' is loosely derived from Kierkegaard's *The Concept of Dread,* trans. Walter Lowrie (Princeton: Princeton University Press, second edition, 1957). Kierkegaard is concerned with the experience of the reality as it breaks in on human beings, or as they flee from it, but he seems to presuppose an understanding of humanness such as I have described.

16. Cf. Peter Berger and Thomas Luckmann, *The Social Construction of Reality* (New York: Doubleday, 1966; paperback edition, 1967).

17. Cf. Herbert McCabe, *What Is Ethics All About?* (Washington: Corpus Press, 1969).

18. *Perspectives on Morality,* p. 145.

Chapter Four

1. For a review of some of the newer methodologies currently in use among Catholic moralists, cf. Charles Curran, "Moral Theology: The Present State of the Discipline," *Theological Studies,* vol. 34, no. 3 (Sept. 19, 1973), 446–67; more specifically, cf. Richard A. McCormick, "Human Significance and Christian Significance," in *Norm and Context in Christian Ethics,* ed. Gene H. Outka and Paul Ramsey (New York: Scribner's, 1968), pp. 237–40.

2. Although not a handbook, *The Dictionary of Moral Theology,* quoted in Chapter One, is an example of the kind of reasoning institutionalized in the handbooks.

3. Frankena sometimes sounds very much like a natural lawyer, e.g., " 'the principles of morality' are something to be *discovered* (or possibly 'revealed'), not something to be created, invented, or decided on by a sheer act of 'decision' or 'commitment' on one's part, as so many seem to think nowadays." "The Principles of Morality" in *Skepticism and Moral Principles,* ed. Curtis L. Carter (Evanston: New University Press, 1973), p. 54.

4. "Natural Law, Tragedy and Theological Ethics," *American Journal of Jurisprudence,* vol. 20 (1975), 1–19.

5. Yet another possible way of proceeding that is not taken here is that which leads to "natural rights." The U.N. Charter on Human Rights, e.g., is usually taken as a natural law document; cf. Bernard Gert, *The Moral Rules* (New York: Harper Torchbooks, 1973), pp. 90–91.

6. H. L. A. Hart, *The Concept of Law* (Oxford: The Clarendon Press, 1961).

7. *Ibid.,* p. 188.

8. *Ibid.,* p. 187.

9. This summary of Hart's position is that given by Ian T. Ramsey in "Toward a Rehabilitation of Natural Law" in *Christian Ethics and Contemporary Philosophy,* ed. Ian T. Ramsey (New York: Macmillan, 1966), pp. 387–88.

10. Hart, *op. cit.,* p. 188.

11. Ian T. Ramsey, *op. cit.,* pp. 388–91, and David Little, "Calvin and the Prospects for a Christian Theory of Natural Law," in *Norm and Context in Christian Ethics,* ed. by Gene H. Outka and Paul Ramsey (New York: Scribner's, 1968), pp. 188–89.

12. Little, *op. cit.,* p. 190.

13. Hart, *op. cit.,* p. 191.

14. *S.T.,* I-II, Q.94, A.6. "There belong to the natural law first certain most general precepts, that are known to all, and secondly certain secondary and more detailed precepts which are, as it were, conclusions following closely from first principles."

15. *S.T.*, I-II, Q.94, A.2.

16. *S.T.*, I-II, Q.94, AA.4, 6.

17. "The decalogue includes those precepts the knowledge of which man has immediately from God. Such are those which with but slight reflection can be gathered at once from the first general principles: and those also which become known to man immediately through divinely infused faith. Consequently two kinds of precepts are not reckoned among the precepts of the decalogue: viz., first general principles, for they need no further promulgation after being once imprinted on the natural reason to which they are self-evident; as, for instance, that one should do evil to no man, and other similar principles;—and again those which the careful reflection of wise men shows to be in accord with reason; as since the people receive these principles from God, through being taught by wise men. Nevertheless both kinds of precepts are contained in the precepts of the decalogue; yet in different ways. For the first general principles are contained in them, as principles in their proximate conclusions; while those which are known through wise men are contained conversely, as conclusions in their principles." *S.T.*, Q.100. A.4.

18. *S.T.*, I-II, Q.100, A.1.

19. *S.T.*, I-II, Q.100, A.8, ad 3.

20. *S.T.*, I-II, Q.95, A.2.

21. *Ibid.*

22. *S.T.*, I-II, Q.94, A.4.

23. *S.T.*, I-II, Q.94, A.4.

24. *S.T.*, I-II, Q.94, A.6.

25. *Ibid.*

26. *S.T.*, I-II, Q.94, A.2.

27. *S.T.*, I-II, Q.95, A.2.

28. "Since the rational soul is the proper form of man, there is in every man a natural inclination to act according to virtue. Consequently, considered thus, all acts of virtue are prescribed by natural law." *S.T.*, I-II, Q.94, A.3.

29. *S.T.*, I-II, Q.94, A.3, ad. 2.

30. Cf. Chapter Two, Footnote 7.

31. *S.T.*, I-II, Q.100, A.1.

32. *S.T.*, I-II, Q.94, A.1.

33. Thomas Aquinas, *Commentary on the Posterior Analytics of Aristotle,* Lecture 20.

34. Wilfrid Sellars, *Science, Perception and Reality* (London: Routledge & Kegan Paul, 1963), p. 317.

35. *Ibid.*, p. 41.

36. *S.T.*, I-II, Q.94, AA.4–6.

37. *S.T.*, I-II, Q.100, A.1.

38. A recent work in this tradition is Bernard Gert's *The Moral Rules* (New York: Harper Torchbook, 1973). The subtitle of the book is descriptive: "A New Rational Foundation for Morality." His work has a good deal in common with Hart's discussion of natural law, but allows more room for the distinctiveness of morals. Hart was chosen for comparison earlier in this chapter because his enumeration of the fundamentals of morality makes more explicit reference to natural law.

39. Cf. Stephen Toulmin, *Human Understanding,* vol. 1. (Princeton: Princeton University Press, 1972).

40. Cf. William A. Clebsch, *American Religious Thought* (Chicago: Chicago University Press, 1973), pp. 144–58.

41. (Garden City: Doubleday, 1966).

42. A very balanced presentation of these themes can be found in Daniel C. Maguire, *The Moral Choice* (Garden City: Doubleday, 1978), especially pp. 261–308.

43. This is a point frequently made by theorists of natural law, cf. e.g., Bruno Schüller: "The fact that the natural moral law concerns him is for man his 'obediential potency' for the fact that the *lex Christi* can concern him." Quoted by Richard A. McCormick, in *Norm and Context in Christian Ethics* (New York: Scribner's, 1968), p. 238.

44. Universalizability has recently come under attack. Gert, e.g., wishes to replace it with a concept of "public advocacy"—a related but not identical concept. He says, "To say that a moral judgment must be one that can be publicly advocated means that the action must be describable in such a way that all rational men understand the kind of action being described. It also means that the action so described must be one toward which it would not be irrational for any man to take the attitude being advocated." *The Moral Rules,* p. 91. Adoption of Gert's position would not seem to radically affect the point I am making.

Chapter 5

1. David Hume, *Treatise on Human Nature,* Book III, Part I, Sec. 1.

2. *Ibid.,* Book I, Part IV, Sec. 7.

3. Cf. Arthur C. Danto, *Mysticism and Morality* (New York: Basic Books, 1972); cf. also *Journal of Religious Ethics,* Vol. 4, No. 1 (Spring, 1976), articles by Wayne Proudfoot, William J. Wainwright, and Arthur C. Danto.

4. *S.T.*, I-II, Q.5, A.8.

5. *Ibid.*

6. *S.T.,* I-II, Q.5, *passim.*

7. *The Trinity and the Unicity of the Intellect,* trans. Sister Rose Em-

manuella Brennan, S.H.N. (St. Louis: Herder & Herder, 1946), Q.IV, A.4, ad.3.

8. Lect. 20, no. 14.

9. *S.T.,* I-II, Q.5, A.3.

10. *S.T.,* I, Q.2, A.1, ad.1.

11. *de Veritate,* Q.10, A.10.

12. *Aquinas and Natural Law* (London: Macmillan, 1967), pp. 23–24.

13. *S.T.,* I-II, Q.114, A.4.

14. *de Veritate,* QQ.16–17.

15. *S.T.,* I, Q.79, A.13.

16. *S.T.,* I-II, Q.94, A.4.

17. *S.T.,* I-II, Q.94, A.1.

18. *Summa Contra Gentiles,* III, Q.129, p. 4. It may no longer be "obvious" that humans have a "determinate nature," but whatever it means to be a human being is true of humans everywhere, which is Thomas' point.

19. (Chicago: University of Chicago Press, 1962, revised edition, 1970).

20. Kuhn, p. 10.

21. Kuhn, p. 69.

22. Kuhn, p. 47.

23. *Commentary on the Posterior Analytics of Aristotle,* Lect. 20.

24. Cf. Preller, pp. 86–88.

25. Sellars, *Science, Perception and Reality,* p. 319.

26. I have in mind here not the fertilization of an ovum in vitro, which has already taken place, but the more drastic case of foetuses raised entirely in laboratories.

27. This point is made in response to John G. Milhaven, "Toward an Epistemology of Ethics," *Theological Studies,* vol. 27, no. 2 (June 1966), 228–241.

28. *de Veritate,* Q.14, A.10.

Index

Anselm, St., 20.
Aristotle, 27, 28, 30, 38, 48, 52, 58, 98, 115.
Augustine, St., 20, 27, 30, 35, 36, 38, 42, 43, 53, 56, 95, 102.
Ayer, A. J., 24, 38.

Barth, Karl, 111, 142.
Becker, Ernest, 19, 20, 67, 68, 139, 142.
Bellah, Robert N., 18, 20.
Bellow, Saul, 75.
Berger, Peter, 104, 124, 143.
Bolt, Robert, 31.
Brown, Norman O., 19, 139.
Buber, Martin, 143.

Cajetan, Cardinal, 27.
Camus, Albert, 16, 139.
Carney, Frederick S., 139.
Clebsch, William A., 146.
Copernicus, 124.
Crowe, Michael B., 138.
Curran, Charles, 144.

Danto, Arthur C., 146.
Darwin, Charles, 67.
D'Entreves, A. P., 138, 139.
Descartes, Rene, 20.
Dunne, John S., 140.

Evans, Donald, 139, 142.

Falk, W. D., 142.
Feuerbach, Ludwig, 104.
Foot, Philippa, 72, 143.
Frankena, William K., 11, 12, 15, 80, 82, 139, 142, 143, 144.
Freud, Sigmund, 77, 78, 79.

Gert, Bernard, 144, 146.
Gödl, Kurt, 14.
Grisez, Germain, 141.

Hart, H. L. A., 83–7, 88, 90, 110, 119, 144.
Hauerwas, Stanley, 82.
Hegel, G. W. F., 20.
Heisenberg, Werner, 14.
Heidegger, Martin, 142.
Hillman, James, 19, 139.
Hobbes, Thomas, 86.
Hume, David, 8, 110, 111, 117, 118, 120, 138, 146.

James, William, 103.
Jefferson, Thomas, 102.

Jerome, St., 48.
John of the Cross, St., 30.

Kant, Immanuel, 17, 18, 50, 98, 99, 108, 118.
Kierkegaard, Soren, 20, 75, 76, 78, 143.
King, Martin Luther, 72.
Kluckholm, Clyde, 86.
Kohlberg, Lawrence, 143.
Kuhn, Thomas S., 124–8, 132, 147.

Lifton, Robert, 19, 139, 142.
Little, David, 86, 144.
Luckmann, Thomas, 104, 124, 143.

Maguire, Daniel C., 12, 15, 108, 146.
Mannheim, Karl, 140.
Marx, Karl, 104.
McCabe, Herbert, 143.
McCormick, Richard A., 144, 146.
Milhaven, John G., 147.
Mill, John Stuart, 102.
Moore, G. E., 8, 11, 65, 138.
Murray, John Courtney, 3, 9, 13, 17, 139.

Newman, John Henry, 27, 53, 140.
Niebuhr, H. Richard, 15.
Nietzsche, Friedrich, 103.

O'Connor, D. J., 119, 120, 121.

Parsons, Talcott, 18.
Pieper, Joseph, 39, 40.
Polanyi, Michael, 18.
Preller, Victor, 40, 41, 97, 140, 141, 147.
Proudfoot, Wayne, 146.

Rahner, Karl, 41.
Ramsey, Ian T., 144.
Rank, Otto, 19, 20.
Rawls, John, 11, 12.
Roberti, Francesco Cardinal, 138.
Ross, James F., 140.
Rieff, Philip, 19, 139, 143.

Schüller, Bruno, 146.
Searle, John R., 138.
Sellars, Wilfred, 97–100, 126, 127, 128, 145, 147.
Soto, Dominic de, 27.
Stevenson, Charles L., 138.
Sturm, Douglas, 27, 140.
Suarez, Francisco, 27.

Thomas Aquinas, St., *Commentary on the Posterior Analytics of Aristotle*, 98, 115, 145, 147; *Commentary on the Sentences of Peter Lombard*, 29, 49, 52, 56, 57, 87, 140, 141; *De Veritate*, 29, 32, 36, 37, 45, 49, 53, 57, 101, 121, 140, 141, 147; *Summa Contra Gentiles*, 53, 57, 142, 147; *Summa Theologiae*, 21, 28, 29, 31, 52, 56–8, 101, 113, 114, 140–3, 145–7; *Supplementum*, 52, 141; *The Trinity*, 114, 146.
Thomas More, St., 31.
Tillich, Paul, 17, 18, 75, 76.
Toulmin, Stephen, 146.
Tracy, David, 139.

Victoria, Francisco de, 27.

Wainwright, William J., 146.